Otter and Dragon
a Love Story

Gloria King

BALBOA.PRESS
A DIVISION OF HAY HOUSE

Balboa Press books may be ordered through booksellers or by contacting:

Balboa Press
A Division of Hay House
1663 Liberty Drive
Bloomington, IN 47403
www.balboapress.com
844-682-1282

Print information available on the last page.

ISBN: 979-8-7652-3999-5 (sc)
ISBN: 979-8-7652-4000-7 (e)

Balboa Press rev. date: 03/15/2023

To Kenneth, my best friend, husband, and loving companion forever, whose strength of character, love, and steadfastness sustains me still. You made me laugh and filled my life with song. You are the one my Soul will always love. You broke my heart, and you healed it. Thank you. All is well.

and

To Gwendolyn Jansma, my Spiritual Mother and Mentor, whose love, support, and guidance changed my life. You are my North Star and my Rock. You opened my heart, taught me to trust, and told me I couldn't do it wrong. You are the wind beneath my wings. Thank you. All is well.

I love you both more than this book or any words can ever encompass, and I hear your laughter often as you plot together endlessly for my higher good. You are written on my Soul. There is no veil between us.

Contents

Acknowledgments ix

Preface xiii

1: The End 1

2: The Dark Night 9

3: The Beginning 17

4: Reflection 37

5: The Search 49

6: The Conjunctio 63

7: Completion 91

8: Beyond the Dark Night 107

9: Transitions 121

10: The Power of Love 131

Afterword 145

Additional Reading 149

Epigraphs 153

Acknowledgments

With Love and Gratitude . . .

To my Editor, Stephanie Kadel Taras without whose friendship, guidance, suggestions, and "due dates" this voyage might never have been completed. You have been my sextant, my anchor, and my sails. May you walk the Beauty Way. Thank you.

and

To my Family, my Friends, and my Sisters of the Heart who held me through the fire, allowed me to walk the road I had to walk without judgment or expectation, grounding me in their love and steadfastness throughout the journey. Blessings to all of you. Thank you.

and

To Spirit, Universe, God-Goddess-All That Is who gave me breath, whose Own Breath whispers in my ear, who lifts me up when I am too broken to fly. Thank You. Thank You. Thank You.

You made your exit
    while my head was turned.
Deliberately I looked at vistas far from you.
Too many unformed words of rage
    stiffened my neck from turning.

You made your exit
    while my feet were kicking at the ropes
    that tied us.
Deliberately I didn't wave goodbye.
My hands were stuffed in pocketfuls of fear.

You made your exit
    while my heart was numb . . .

It took me years to realize
    I could not say goodbye to you
    until, deliberately, I'd said hello.

— Gwendolyn Jansma, from
    "Detour" in *Gwenana – Her Words*

Preface

When I think back on those early days of Ken and me, of the days of bliss, I recall several things that stand out as defining, forming the essence of Otter and Dragon. There were some ordinary and extraordinary moments quite early on that established a pattern for us and now permeate my memory of our time together, identifying for me who we were as a couple: eye-to-eye, holding hands, oneness and twoness, the vesica pisces, otter and dragon.

The first I noticed almost immediately. From the start, we always looked at each other directly, eye to eye, when we talked. This habit dissipated some over time, of course, but always returned when the conversation held a particular level of importance. This was a habit I had often noticed with my spiritual mentor, Gwen Jansma, how she greeted people with this direct, eye-to-eye gaze that seemed to connect our souls and seal those energies together. It was a bonding process that I've not often experienced; as a culture, we tend to be not very good at looking directly at each other. I know I feel that way, and I've always had trouble doing that, except with Gwen – and Ken.

The next was spending time hand-in-hand. Holding hands just came naturally, was never awkward. This is an ordinary thing; many couples hold hands. But again, it had never been my experience, so it came as a delicious surprise to me that he would just take my hand so often – sitting on the sofa talking, driving in the car, walking down the street, lying in bed, each reading a book (though it made turning the pages a little tricky at first).

"Oneness and Twoness," well that was a conversation topic we returned to many times. I have no memory of how it started. Much the same as many of our conversations, I suspect. One of us would ponder some idea or statement out loud and then we just wandered around in it for a while together. Sometimes, we never really got to the end of what something held for us; such was the case of Oneness and Twoness, as we kept finding new ways to look at it.

It began, I believe, with a pondering of the oneness that was each of us and the twoness of what was growing between us. Most of my life I had spent in a lifestyle of oneness, having been a single woman at that point for 30 years. Although I had been in relationships since my divorce in 1982, I had always lived alone and had enjoyed it, preferred it. On the other hand, Ken had almost always been part of a twoness, having married out of college and then remarried again after the break-up of his first marriage. I had come into his life well after his second marriage was over, but with two young adult kids still living at home, he'd really never had much of a single life.

It had come as a surprise to him that he could experience singleness, oneness, within our twoness. I encouraged him to be on his own when he wanted, to go play golf with a buddy or create a place where he could be alone in the house once we lived together. I've never been a "joined at the hip" kind of gal, I guess, and he came to appreciate that as he discovered he enjoyed having time to himself, a luxury he had never even known he wanted or could have before. For me, the surprise came with the acknowledgement that I did indeed like closeness, twoness, cuddling on the couch instead of sitting in my own chair, having the same someone actively in my life every single day, making decisions together, going to bed at night together and snuggling together the next morning as a start to each day.

Once we had comfortably recognized oneness within twoness, and vice versa, within our relationship, we progressed to a twoness within Oneness. It was a theological conversation I suppose that in a simplistic way went something like this: We are individuals with something we call free will, each unique, like snowflakes, yet, we are one with God and all sentient beings and so also part of a twoness. A dichotomy of sorts that is difficult to define – twoness within the oneness. And while we intellectually accept – perhaps embrace – the idea of "the other" in our world, if we are one with All, then there is no other. But we're still individuals, right? So, oneness within twoness within The Oneness? And life is full of oneness and twoness by virtue of the multiplicity of our relationships. Eventually, we laughed over our circular thinking: Sooo, I'm an individual (oneness) within the twoness of any relationship, within the oneness of the specific group, within the twoness of a larger group, within the Oneness of God. We kept adding layers of examples of the oneness within the twoness within the oneness and . . . well, it often went on and on like that with a somewhat undefinable endpoint. Maybe you had to be there, but you get the drift. It was a long and complicated string that became difficult to keep track of sometimes, but it was a conversation we comfortably and lightheartedly returned to time and time again, enjoying the somewhat holographical picture it painted.

When coupled with my dabbling in Numerology, attention continued to be returned to that conversation, noticing that quite frequently something in our lives reduced itself numerologically to a one or a two, or had some significance around ones or twos. Most notably, one day I was doing the numerology on our names and discovered that his name had no ones and my name had no twos. We came to the conclusion that this was a reflection of our earlier discussions of Ken's always having been part of a pair or group in life and me quite single in my process over the years, even when in relationships or groups, and how, especially once we were married, we were together now, and each provided that missing piece, the missing number, for the other. Uh oh, here we go again.

This brings me to the shape known in Sacred Geometry as the vesica-pisces. It is formed when two overlapping circles with the same radius meet, such that the edge of each touches the center of the other, forming a sort of eye shaped area that is shared by both circles. Each circle has its own space, as well as the shared space with the other. Two wedding rings are often depicted this way, and with the oneness and twoness of our relationship firmly established, the symbolism easily fit into our conversations. Just as with the vesica-pisces, each of our edges had touched the heart, the center, of the other, and the soft, loving space shared between us allowed for the individuality of our outer circles to remain intact. I associated that symbol with us, our picture of togetherness and included it in my wedding vows.

So what about "Otter and Dragon," you may be asking? Well, the Dragon comes as a natural totem for me, as you will read more about later. Dragons have complicated and layered nuances to their personas, but in general they tend to be seen as magical, mercurial, powerful, elusive, protective, and a force of nature with a capacity for wisdom. They are also a symbol of spiritual alchemy. Beneficent in some cultures and fearsome in others, dragons, within a bond of trust, are an ally like no other. For me, dragons embody both attributes that I think of as mine, as well as those that I aspire toward. They make me feel happy and safe and every bit as magical as they are.

Ken became "Otter" m any y ears before I met him. It happened o n a daddy-daughter weekend with Stephanie for her Indian Princess group. Very simply, it was an animal totem he took as part of a ceremony there. The "medicine" held by otter is both tender and playful. Otter is very caring of its young and family; it's also curious, friendly, joyous, bright, and adventuresome; everyone is otter's friend until proven otherwise.

I have no idea if Ken knew any of this when he took on the name, but he personified all of these attributes in both his personal and business life. As truth often does, the name stuck once he brought it home, and there were a number of Otter Christmas ornaments and other otter keepsakes in his collection to commemorate it. Otter and Dragon became an obvious choice for the title of this book when I saw the symbology hinting at what lay in our core beings as a confirmation that two distinctly different individuals can find commonality, love, and a sense of oneness within the twoness of each other.

As to the "why" of writing this book, I have to say that at the outset, I just knew I had to do it. I knew it was primarily for me. It was a means of confirming my own journey through what I can only call a Dark Night of the Soul, as I grieved for what seemed insurmountable losses – the loss of the love of my life whom I'd only just found at age sixty and had known for only twenty-two months, the loss of what had been my "adult" relationship with God, and the loss of my illusions about love and life, all leaving me quite empty for a time.

Later, as I meandered through my discoveries and began to look deeper into what propelled me to the writing, I found a larger scope, a bigger umbrella if you will: the desire to share more of my spiritual self with loved ones who hadn't known much about that side of me.

Throughout my life, I've struggled with allowing myself to be seen, for those close to me to really know me, to allow myself to be that vulnerable. Over the years, I found a spiritual sisterhood that has supported such sharing, and I've opened more within that circle but that was the exception rather than the rule. When I met Ken, it was the first time I had trusted a man so deeply and opened myself up so early and so completely in the relationship, and that trust was never betrayed. Having Ken in my life gave me a sense of inner freedom I've rarely known.

This book then initially became an attempt to share at a deeper level with those beyond that small circle. There have always been those in my life with whom I felt less comfortable sharing my less-than-traditional spiritual leanings, and I came to see this book as an opportunity to express more openly and fully who I am. This book gives me a chance to offer a piece of myself, to share cliff notes on my life and my experience of Ken's passing, of our relationship before and after death, and of my own spiritual journey, with the hope that it will all be accepted as a part of who I am. I wanted to live a more authentic life, be more true to the whole of myself. What has become routine, the spiritual thread that runs through each and every day for me, has not always been easy to explain. So what better way than to write this book about my journey with Ken as a way to capture what is often difficult to do in conversation?

Further investigation into my motives, my reasons for this undertaking, led me to a second realization: this book may give me the cathartic experience my soul still needs. It is one thing to come through a dark night experience and have a knowing on the other side as to the meaning, method, or message of that journey. It is quite another to choose to articulate it in some way for others, and, through that effort, come to know and understand that journey on an entirely different level for oneself. While I had gone through the various stages of grief and had plowed through a process that brought me not only to my knees, but to an acceptance and even an appreciation of what happened, there was still a need for closure, to solidify my beliefs in some different way, to capture what I had learned from a different perspective. This book has been my means to that end, and the insights have never stopped coming, even well after the completion of this book.

It was only much later that I came to the third notion, that this book might benefit others who stumble on it in some way; perhaps some larger good might be done through the sharing of my experiences. It is my sincere hope that in whatever way this book has called to you, in whatever way it has whispered your name, it provides what you need to hear in this moment to assist you with your own dark journey, whether past, present, or future, and to affirm that there is always a light at the end of the tunnel. I truly believe that by putting one foot in front of the other you will eventually and most certainly find it. Or perhaps it will find you.

The journey of writing this book has been a long one, and one who's path and direction has changed countless times along the way. There have been interruptions and halts that have served me, offering opportunities to look again at what it was I intended to achieve by such an undertaking and what I was actually trying to convey of my own experiences over these last few years.

This book represents a distillation of what has taken me thus far in my lifetime to digest and integrate into my own being. From my five-year old self in church to literally dreaming this book; from being at the mountaintop with Ken, to being in the depths of despair without him, it took all of that and everything in between to assure that integration into a more whole self. It has brought me to a place of knowing how strong I really am, what it is that truly supports me, and that it is always an ongoing process of choice and change. Ken was a gift to me, and his loss a gift to my soul. The experience of writing this book has nourished me and encouraged me in ways I could not have imagined at the start. May it do so for you as well.

> *"The journey of grief is as individual as a fingerprint. Although the intensity, depth, and duration can be overwhelming and seemingly endless, it is an invitation of the Soul . . . After a loved one dies, our Souls need to journey deep within the void and discover . . . the great abyss of the unknown. Within that darkness, there is always light. How you find the light in the dark can be for some the beginning of the authentic self. May we all have the courage to dive in deeply and twist and turn in our discomfort, as it is within this very distress we begin to find a new and profound relationship with our Soul."*

> – Austyn Wells (AustynWells.com)

1

The End

The stone of death
dropped in a family pond
makes tidal waves
and leaves a hole as large as Earth.

Death visits in many guises. It takes on different personalities, unique to the situation at hand, yet often looking quite similar to casual observation. They are as diverse as snowflakes, just as we are all different from each other, unlike anything that has come before or after. The methods of joining with Death are many. It comes suddenly or through a long and lingering sunset; in solitude or with pause enough to have loved ones gathered; quietly or with torrents of emotion, whether spewing a whirlwind of resistance or simply amping up the energy required to leave the body and go Home. Whatever the method, the recipe yields something different every time. The energy in the room varies greatly; we are alone, or with someone, or with a roomful of others. We add our own carefully orchestrated exit. Those involved are having their own emotions, experiences, and memories, and they bring to the mix their history, attitudes, beliefs about death, fears perhaps, and other baggage of their own.

I've seen the process of death play out numerous times, over the last twenty years in particular. Sometimes present at the moment of passing and sometimes not, I've experienced the parting of parents, grandparents, aunts, uncles, cousins, friends, mentors, and pets. Despite the number of times we have the experience, we never get used to it, perhaps *because* it is never the same. But it is an honor to be present when Death appears, to not only give comfort, but to bear witness to an experience as sacred and ancient as time itself. It can have a certain quiet to it, a peaceful space to lean into. And if we can stay open in those moments as witness, we may even be given a very special gift.

October 10, 2009

The week before Ken died, I was casually walking across the kitchen to fetch something for him when I glanced at the calendar hanging on the end of my cupboards. A full-on head shot of a beautiful tiger looked back at me from the picture, capturing me with intense, yet gentle eyes. My attention instantly caught on October 18.

I noticed that it was to be a New Moon, but more importantly, the date held me in the same way the tiger's eyes had held me, and I could not look away. I can't explain this experience, but it needed no interpretation. I knew it was the day Ken would die.

At that moment, I was curiously compliant, without heightened emotion of any kind. When presented with such a Knowing, how can one react in any other way but with calm surrender? Yet, as the days quietly slipped by, I could feel myself trying to put my foot on the brake of the now racing locomotive of Time.

I continued with my care of Ken as usual, and sometime that week, Ken's good friend, Mike, arrived, offering to stay for a few days to give me a chance to rest and sleep. As an M.D., I suppose he had an understanding of Ken's condition and knew he was there to say his goodbyes as well, but at the outset, when we had set up those dates, we did not know how imminent Ken's death would become. Mike was a Godsend. He was so kind and caring with Ken, and to me. Later, I would realize how much I appreciated his gracious and unselfish act. It was his loving presence that allowed me the time I needed to center myself for what was to come.

October 17, 2009

Mike left quietly when Ken's sisters came in from Illinois. Son Brian and wife Jenn came in from Ohio. Stephanie and her new husband, Kevin, lived nearby and joined us too. Though no one said the words, that evening we all settled in for the final wait.

Ken's youngest, John, couldn't be there. I felt badly for John most of all, as Ken had been his rock. Stephanie at least had Kevin now, but John seemed to have no one to lean on. I felt his aloneness deeply and sent a little prayer his way. An unusual quiet came over me then, surrounding my heart and cloaking the charged emotions beginning to well up inside.

A LOVE STORY

It was an odd mix of energy in the house. Up to this time, I'd barely spent any time at all with Ken's sisters. The same was true with Brian and Jenn.

Save for a couple of brief meetings, the trip to Florida Ken and I had spent with them and the kids, and the times Brian had visited during Ken's illness, there had been little time to get to know each other, though it had been nearly two years. And even though Stephanie and Kevin lived nearby, the time we had spent together was also negligible, given the situation we now found ourselves in. We thought there would be plenty of time. Just four months ago, we had all been more or less living our day to day lives, oblivious to how little time there was left.

And now, here I was in a room full of near strangers, but in my own home, our home. Ken, our common heartstring, was woven in and around and through all of us. We were here to say goodbye to this man we loved so much. Yet here I was, his wife, feeling rather the outsider, as though his being in this house was only circumstantial, as his "family" gathered around. It was certainly not at all the case, not the way they felt about me, but merely the general isolation I was feeling, knowing what was to come. Perhaps we all were in that same space.

I honestly don't remember much about what happened earlier in the day. I think there was food that people had brought for us. I recall a few other visitors dropping by, or maybe that was the day before. It's all just a blur really. What I do remember is how quiet it seemed in the house, despite the number of people around.

Ken was lying in a hospice bed in the living room, in front of the fireplace, under the painting of Grandmother Moon. This was where we had talked for hours in the early days, where we had first kissed, where we had made love in front of the fireplace one blustery winter night, where we had said our wedding vows . . . where he was going to die.

In the afternoon the family spent time taking care of him, talking to him. I wanted to give them space to do so privately, so I came into the room for only a few moments here and there. At one point I was sitting on the sofa next to his bed, and Ken's sister, bless her, must have perceived some need in me that I was not even aware of at the time. She quietly suggested I slip onto the bed with him so I could hold him one last time. All the awkwardness I had been feeling that day melted away as I eased myself onto the bed with Ken and put my arms around him. I kissed his cheek and, holding his hand, rested there for a while, my head nestled into his shoulder, a place that had once yielded such comfort and safety.

Ken said very little during those last couple of days. We were giving him morphine for pain which kept him pretty drowsy and out of it for the most part. Later that afternoon, however, he seemed more alert for a short time. At some point, he called for me. When I came to his side, he took my hand. With his other hand, he pointed toward the doorway into the kitchen. "Look!" he said with some animation. "Look, see that light over there? Can you bring it over here for me? Can you bring it closer?"

I murmured that I thought he was the only one who could do that. "I think you can do it without even getting out of bed," I said. He seemed to understand, smiled wanly, and went silent for a time.

Sometime later he announced that his suitcase was all packed for his trip but he couldn't find his passport. "Can you help me find it?" he asked. I assured him I would, and then added, "Oh, it's right here, Honey, whenever you're ready." He quieted again. I think it was the last thing I ever heard him say.

Day relinquished itself to the night. Ken's breathing became much slower, and more shallow. While it seemed he sometimes knew we were there, he did not open his eyes again or speak.

Then, without anyone discussing it, the ritual began. One by one, each person present began to take their last moments with Ken. The rest of us sat around the dining room table talking softly. I was already in a strange fog, hearing little, feeling little, aware of little around me. I waited until everyone had completed their goodbyes; then I sat with him for a while and inexplicably found myself quietly singing "Amazing Grace" as he slept – the same verse, over and over. He'd never specifically mentioned that song as a favorite, but I somehow felt these were the words he now needed to hear. In retrospect, perhaps I needed to hear them too.

> Through many dangers, toils, and snares
> I have already come.
> 'Tis grace that brought me safe thus far,
> And grace will lead me home.

By then it was late. Seeing no change in him, I suggested we should all try to get some sleep; I'd stay on the couch and let everyone know if anything happened. Stephanie and Kevin went home; the rest were staying with me, so all went to bed and tried to sleep. Midnight arrived, and with it the date that had shown itself so prominently on the calendar just a week earlier.

October 18, 2009
12:30 a.m.

The house is quiet and totally dark. Blinds have been drawn, and there is no discernible light. It is all-encompassing, and the level of darkness matches my gloom as I sit with Ken, listening intently to his barely detectable breath. There is a sense of awe in the back of my mind as I recall the strong inner knowing a week ago that today would mark his passing, and I sadly acknowledge its accuracy. I'm sure it won't be long now, and I settle in on the couch, wide-awake. Ken becomes a bit vocal, although I cannot quite make out the words he is saying. Restless too, his feet are moving under the covers. He's not really sleeping, but not really *here* either. In a single breath, my head begins to swim a bit and my eyelids become uncontrollably heavy and I feel myself slip away into an unwilling sleep.

2 a.m.

I awake with a start. I thought I heard something in the dining room; maybe Brian got up to see how Ken was doing. I sit up to look in that direction. The sound of someone moving across the dining room floor toward the kitchen is clear. A bit groggy, but alert to the noise, I look towards the kitchen, toward that same doorway where Ken had seen the light only hours earlier. The room, though sitting within the deep darkness of this night, seems slightly illuminated at that doorway in nearly colorless shades of sepia and gray. And there, standing just inside the kitchen door, I see a VERY TALL Being. He is cloaked and loosely hooded yet somehow full of light. I can see no features. He seems quite oblivious to me, focused completely on Ken. As he begins to move forward, he has to duck down considerably in order to come through the doorway. Moving soundlessly to the bed he stands like a guardian at Ken's feet. His essence is reverent in nature – benevolent, compassionate.

At that moment, the room *fills* with beings so soft and encompassing, like formless angels holding the space for the sacred ceremony now underway. I cannot see them, but I can feel their presence most

5

definitely. The room becomes quite warm, and the air I breathe is thick. They continue to come, crowding into every corner of the room. I feel the beat of my own heart within this ethereal energy. Wordless questions on my lips, I remain still and quiet, trying to take it all in by some osmosis-like process.

But, again, sleep comes over me like a heavy veil that I cannot resist, despite all my efforts to do so. Wanting so much to stay with Ken and these Beings, and fighting the loss of consciousness even as I feel it slipping from my grasp, I fall away once again, as though drugged. Spirit bars my presence during The Preparation.

3 a.m.

I awake once more with suddenness, as though shaken by some unseen hand. Ken is still breathing, but very slowly. The air remains thick, and an energy I can only call Love – though it seemed much, much more than that – is now present in the room.

The Tall One stands steadfastly at Ken's feet, as I, the voyeur, try in vain to continue my own vigil. But again, I am compelled to sleep. Though I want to take Ken's hand and speak to him, my body, weighed down by some unseen presence, gives up. I am unable to move or resist. My mind whispers "no, please, not now," as they send me into yet another deep sleep.

4 a.m.

My eyes open. I am wide awake, alert, on guard, the previous heaviness having instantly lifted. I am tuned immediately to my surroundings and aware of a need to be present – *right now!* Chills go up my spine and little hairs on my neck and arms stand on end. Something tells me not to move. I wait, barely allowing myself to even breathe.

4:10 a.m.

I listen closely. Ken's breathing has changed. It comes cautiously now, hesitating, with long pauses between exhale and inhale. I hold my own breath with his and, with my own inhale, *will* him to do the same – but he is no longer mine. Ken is barely present, on the precipice, moving through, and letting go. I take his hand – already cool to the touch – and try in vain to warm it, holding it close to my heart. I tell him I am right there and that I love him, and that it is OK to go . . . and, without hesitation, he floats away from his body like dandelion fluff on the breath, as though he had waited for me to speak, for my touch, before doing so.

The room immediately clears with a soft yet focused . . . *swooooop!*

All I had experienced, all that had been there, including the Tall One, the warm Angelic Ones, and Ken, were, in an instant, lifted up into what seemed like a gentle cosmic vortex and returned to Source. I felt for a brief second that I could go with him part of the way but missed making that split-second decision, and remained consciously in the room. The warm thickness that had been pervasive was gone, and a coolness took its place. I was awake and alert, no longer under the anesthesia of Spirit. It was over.

I realized that I had been holding my breath for some appreciable amount of time; my chest was tight, holding on somehow to those moments. A sharp intake of some much needed oxygen and I was back on the planet again, landing in a reality that left me disoriented. I spent a few precious moments with Ken, unable to fully comprehend what I had been allowed to witness.

I soon realized, however, that I couldn't take the extra time I so desperately wanted with this experience. There were others here who loved Ken, and their needs required attention as well. I woke Brian and they woke the others. Stephanie was called. Someone phoned John. When we were gathered again and all had taken the time they needed, the dutiful release of the body was made. I would pick up his ashes later that week.

There was a surreal passage of time at that point. The fact that his body was so suddenly *not* there was disconcerting and troublesome. It felt like I was in some bubble hovering in the area, observing but not seeing. Listening but not hearing. Present but not there at all, watching from some other vantage point what was happening.

After a few hours everyone prepared to leave, to return to their own lives to grieve in their own ways. The earlier sense of being strangers had dissipated now, tethered together as we were by the experience of Ken's death. We had been through the same fire together and, for me, there was a sense of unwillingness to cut that cord. I didn't really want them to go so soon, but I felt powerless to say anything. I couldn't cry; I couldn't talk. I could barely move. I was numb. I was exhausted. I couldn't begin to comprehend what had happened or what to do next. Nothing was real, yet nothing had ever been so agonizingly painful and tangible.

Someone, Brian and Jenn I think, called one of my friends before they left so I wouldn't be alone. I went to the bedroom to lie down for a while and was curled up in a fetal position when I heard the doorbell ring. Brian and Jenn sent her back to my room. She stood in the doorway briefly, just looking at me, unsure of her next step, I suppose. I don't remember if she said anything at all, but likely she knew that no words could possibly help. She walked around to the other side of the bed and slipped up behind me, put her arm around me, and held me spoon-like, much like Ken used to do as we drifted off to sleep.

I still couldn't cry; the tears were stuck somewhere. But I was sobbing uncontrollably on the inside. She offered me the only comfort I was to feel for a very long time, and I was so grateful for her tender compassion.

2

The Dark Night

Say what you will,
your words don't keep my feet on solid ground.
I'm drowning in my pain.

Say I must eat,
and I must sleep
and I must go on living.
Say what you will,
your words don't keep my feet on solid ground.
...I'm drowning in my pain.

I awoke the next morning, lying on the couch in the living room. I remembered heading to bed the night before and, walking into the bedroom, took one look at the empty bed, turned around and left, unable to stay there. I slept on the couch, if you could call it sleeping, but managed, I suppose, to get something akin to rest in the long hours between dusk and dawn. I hadn't written in my journal much in the preceding weeks but picked it up now, intending to capture my experience of the night Ken died.

What spilled off the point of my pen first was not only unexpected, but filled the next several pages as though written by some unseen hand. I wrote like a child just learning to print; the words were huge and the letters misshapen, written with such force that they literally ripped through the paper in a few places. The pain of my disbelief was raw, as mere words tried in vain to capture the grief I felt. Rage spilled out onto the page in relentless torrents until I was spent, leaving nothing but a hollow in the pit of my stomach, and the sentient emptiness of the house, of my heart.

Anguish flooded my body as I dropped the pen to grab my stomach and bend over in agony, releasing a silent scream. Alternating between not breathing at all and taking in huge gulps amid the sobs I found myself screaming at the ceiling, *"No! Yesterday we were laughing and in love! Yesterday we got married! Yesterday we were planning our FUTURE! I waited my whole life to find him and now – now – he is gone? DEAD?!!! NO! NO! NO!"*

> *"Grief wraps its arms around my knees*
> *as a fearful child*
> *who will not be left behind."*

—Gwenana, from "Grief" in *Arrows To The Heart*

The loss was too much to bear, and I was unable to find any way to either quiet or endure what was going on inside. No amount of "NO" could bring him back. While I did write of my experience of Ken's passing, all peace I might have been able to embrace from the mystical experience at his death was gone; the only thing I knew was the pain. I retreated to a semi-numb state, and the rest of the day was a blur of emptiness and disbelief as I distanced myself from the tangle of emotions beginning to build inside me.

I alternately slipped more fully into grief or denial as time began its slow transition between "then" and "now." The stages of grief came out of order, upside down, inside out, overlapping, and recurring. There was no solid ground any more, no way to make sense of, or make peace with, what had happened, no way to subside the rumbling beginning to reverberate from deep within.

An earthquake was about to erupt within me.

With the next day came the relative normalcy of activity. There were things to be done. I needed to go out for cat food; I bought the inevitably needed Thank-You cards; I needed stamps, and did some laundry, all enabling me to stay busy and remain in semi-denial, retaining the numbness as a shield against the coming emotional storm.

Anger knocked on my door on the fourth day. Some friends, my "Gateways sisters," a spiritual group I belonged to and close women friends I'd known for years, made an attempt to gather and offer me an evening of sisterhood and ceremony. Although it felt too soon at the time and I should have listened to my gut and declined, I had agreed to their suggestion, and they arrived at the house on Wednesday evening.

We went downstairs to the area where we had offered sacred ceremony for others so many times before; where we welcomed the last of the Heartseek Gatherings with Gwen before she retired; where we had hosted workshops with many other spiritual teachers over the years. It's a large room, seating twenty or more. Soft, neutral colors set the tone, comfy, welcoming couches, with artwork and artifacts reflecting my spiritual sensibilities: a picture of women dancing around a fire; Native American symbols in paintings and shelf-sitters; books on various spiritual practices and the like. Big windows at the back of the house frame a natural wetland area full of grasses and cattails with a wooded area behind that. These were all surroundings that had given me nurturance in the past. That night, candlelight cast a warm glow, and yet I was cold – physically, mentally, emotionally, and most of all, spiritually.

My recollection is vague but I fear I behaved quite badly that night. The anger was beginning to rise as we formed the circle. I was not angry at them, I just didn't want to be there, didn't want to acknowledge the situation; didn't feel Spirit and didn't want to. Anger. Anger that we should be gathering here, for this reason, and for me to seriously expect, let alone want, solace from Spirit! My frame of mind was that of spitting on the ground in disgust. Solace? From the very God that took Ken from me? This two-faced being who gifted me with this sweet, sweet love, then turned on me and took it back just as I had begun to truly trust that it was real. Yeah, I was angry. And it was just beginning, just the tip of the iceberg. The tone of the voice in my head was cold and spiteful and full of venom.

I recall being sullen and making a couple of unkind and sharp remarks, saying that no one could possibly understand what I was going through, despite knowing that each of these women had experienced heartaches of their own in the past. The evening ended early, it being quite clear that I hadn't been ready for this. Bless their understanding hearts that they continued to support me in other ways through these dark early days and on into a future that I could not yet see.

Day Five, Stephanie and I meet at my house to put together two Memory Boards to sit in the lobby of the church sanctuary during the upcoming Saturday memorial. I found the time spent with Stephanie very comforting. I hadn't been sure what to expect really, not knowing her very well, but I found this time to be lovely. Not easy, but lovely. It kept me busy on a task, for one thing, filling a hole in time and getting me on to some sort of next step in this dismal process. I don't remember talking very much, but talk seemed unnecessary. Our wordlessness did not mean no communication. I felt very much in tune with her that day and surprisingly peaceful, given where I had been the evening before.

We had lots of pictures of Ken from his early days as a laboratory researcher, to his young fatherhood, to corporate successes, to family gatherings . . . to Gloria and Ken – our many trips together, building the closet in the basement together, our wedding. We had found some printed quotes on vellum notepads, and other stickers from craft projects which were used as meaningful asterisks here and there on the boards, things we felt best described him as a father, a husband, a man. So much love went into those boards that I knew it would be felt by anyone who really took the time to look at them. I believe Stephanie and I began a bond that day, in the love and pain that we shared, as we placed our hearts into all that we created to express it.

On Day Six, I went to pick up Ken's ashes. I waited in a quiet, nicely appointed room with comfortable overstuffed chairs and a sofa, serene pictures, soft colors, and muted lighting; a suitably calming sitting room, considering the circumstances. A kind gentleman in a dark suit and tie entered and introduced himself. He explained that the ashes were ready and if I would pick out a container, the ashes would be put into the container for me. He left me alone for a few minutes while I looked at several urns in a cabinet. Some metallic, some wood, some ceramic and painted in different designs. Though I did not like any of them, in the end I finally chose a very simple woodgrain box, feeling that Ken would not want anything showy or ornate. A couple of minutes later the gentleman in the dark suit brought it back to me, heavy now, and I took Ken home.

Day Seven, the day of Ken's service had come. Family arrived, and we headed out for Ken's church to say a last goodbye and honor his life. I had written something to say the day before, and now it was all about going through the motions, just getting through it. I almost had Jenn read my words for me, having a sense that if I had to use my voice I would break down completely. Finally, I found my courage and spoke, in the end needing to express my love and my experience of this extraordinary man. Measure 4 Measure, a men's choral group that Ken had belonged to, was there and sang some of Ken's favorites from their repertoire. I was overcome by how many people showed up, those from Ken's business life as well as friends and family, and those who came for me, some who'd never even met him. I was left in awe by it all.

All the words were spoken, songs were sung, luncheon completed, people thanked. It had become such a familiar routine from past funerals I'd been a part of that, at moments, I almost forgot this was for Ken, my beloved Ken, and was taken by surprise a little when condolences were offered, forgetting that I was the widow now, the one left behind and in sorrow. The pain of that recognition would hit later when I was finally, really alone

That night, I went to the website that had been created in memory of Ken. I read some of the posts and listened to the music that I'd asked to be linked in, including one of our favorite John Denver songs, "Perhaps Love."

As I listened to the familiar song, the memories flooded in: the first time he played this song for me during those new days and weeks after we met, dancing to it at our wedding only four months earlier, and then an evening about a year before, near his birthday, when we had danced in my living room, just swayed mostly, and he'd sung the lyrics softly in my ear. I could still feel his arms around me, my head nestled into his shoulder, the scent of him filling my senses. As the song ended, I whispered along with the words, ". . . if I should live forever and all my dreams come true, my memories of love will be of you."

Looking at the pictures on the Memory Boards now sitting in my living room that were so full of life, and holding his ashes close, suddenly, the dam that had been holding back the tears that whole week finally broke, and I cried uncontrollably for the first time. Once started it seemed they would never stop, and it felt like hours before, exhausted, I fell into an uneasy sleep.

———————∞∞∞———————

". . . and all that's left
    are salty tears I want to catch and save.
    Just to have something."

—Gwenana, from "Divorce" *in Inverted Trees*

———————∞∞∞———————

This seemingly unending week had finally come to a close. Time had plodded along in some slow-motion, dream-like bubble, but now it was over . . . and another would begin. The whole week had been permeated with darkness and gilded by the dull edge of an ashen ache. There was to be a plethora of unending aches before I would feel life seeping back into my bones or any real light go on in the darkness.

Where Are You?

The days that followed were very quiet; the house was quiet and empty feeling; the very space around me was empty, barren. There was a pervasive aloneness that permeated my whole being. It encompassed me. It lived in every inch of my skin, my mind, my blood, my bones, in every cell. Once all the ceremony was over, the service completed, the family gone home, cards received, thank you notes written, there was nowhere else to hide. Ken was gone. I had no signals that he was anywhere around, no sense within me that he still existed or had ever existed. Nights were the worst. No dreams of him when I did manage to sleep but most of those hours were spent in a restlessness that fell just short of sleep. Mostly I slept on the sofa, unable to bear being in the bed we had shared from the beginning with such joy. And often realizing that I was lying in roughly the same space he had occupied when he died. Rest was impossible; there was no place that did not remind me of Ken. Many days went by when I never made it out of my robe, and the crying and ranting at God became the norm; I was enraged and sometimes totally out of control, screaming at the heavens. It had been a betrayal in the worst possible way.

One day after the next, after the next, unending next days . . . he was gone, completely gone, and his silence thundered in my ears. I strained to hear his voice, called out to him to come to me in any way he could. Nothing.

The emptiness was palpable. Was death really so absolute? I'd never experienced this before. Mom and Dad had both come to me in symbols and dreams, and very soon after their passing. I'd known they were still with me, felt their presence, heard their messages. But this . . . this piercing silence. Had it all been some figment of my imagination? Worse, had our love even been real? I was doubting it. For surely, if it had been real, I would have heard from him, wouldn't I? I'd never felt so utterly alone and unsure of what had once been so solid. I could barely breathe in the thin atmosphere of my loneliness and confusion.

About two weeks after the service, I had a session with a local healer and shaman. One thing in particular stood out. She mentioned that it usually takes the dead about forty days to acclimate to their new surroundings before they have the capacity to connect in some way with loved ones here on the earth plane. With this simple statement, *hope*, just the tiniest little ember of hope was kept alive.

And while I began a count of the days, a sameness took over my life. The blending of one day into the next became a routine. Days with no purpose, no future, no joy, and time – endless time – with no change, no movement, no life. I fed the cats and, I suppose, myself. I met with friends, participated in the usual activities, but I was just going through the motions. I may have looked like I was healing and moving on, but I was actually still living in a fog of grief, anger, despair, and a sense of futility.

Then came an event that began the change. Ken's phone still sat on the kitchen counter in an organizer where we had always kept and charged both of our phones. I needed to keep seeing it there. I'd kept it charged, telling myself that I would let it go once I had retrieved some information from it – mostly addresses and phone numbers of his friends and relatives that I'd never added to my own address book. I just couldn't do that yet, so I left his phone sitting there, at once a painful reminder and a bittersweet comfort.

That day, on impulse, I picked it up and began to look through some of the information and found myself looking at his list of recent phone calls. Morbid curiosity perhaps, but who had been the last few people he had called and talked to? Listed there was his friend and lawyer, Jim; son, Brian; friend and accountant, Claire. All calls made back in early September. And then there was Gloria, the last one, *on October 19 – the day after Ken died.* Thoughts raced through my mind. I had been alone at home that whole day, and obviously there had been no phone call from Ken.

Incredulous and stunned, I took a sharp breath in and looked steadily at the phone's screen for some time, expecting it to change, for my eyes to clear and find that this inexplicable sight had dissolved. I blinked and held my breath, fearing that even such a small movement would somehow change what I was seeing. But it didn't. My eyes happened to catch the pages of the calendar on the counter and quickly did the math; it was 43 days since Ken's passing.

It was the first glimmer of a thaw. He had called. He had sent a message that he was still with me! This was the sign I had been yearning for. He was saying "hello, I'm still here!" He had found a way to send me a message. There is no logical explanation for the existence of that call on his phone (or that I just happened to look there for that matter), but logic does not always hold the answers. For the first time in a long while, the ache lessened just a bit. The tears that constantly filled the space behind my eyes dissipated. A tentative peace overrode my sorrow as I savored that precious discovery.

My spirit would waiver many times after that, and I would continue to fall into major bouts of anger and depression, but this was the first turning point, however tenuous, on the journey back to life. A modicum of hope had returned and with it a rush of memories that filled me with a desire to reconnect with Ken, and that would fuel many months of immersion into a journey far bigger than I could imagine.

3

The Beginning

You know those years of life
politely labeled 'golden'?

I wonder.
Will you use that time to stand in love?
I am.
My lover's skin and mine
respectfully stand side by side
encouraging the other to expand.
I call this coming home.

It is summer 2007. For quite some time, at least months prior, if not years, Gwen, my spiritual mentor had been telling me that romance was not over in my life. That there was more to come and that it would not happen until I came to acknowledge within myself that I truly did want that again, and when I became clear just what it was that I wanted.

I had toyed with the idea, unsure first of all if she was right, and second, whether or not I really wanted to risk it again. Never lucky in love, my relationships had always been either disastrous, or ill timed (or both), and I had felt for some ten years now that it was pointless to try again. From my first marriage through other long-term relationships, it had seemed to repeatedly have been the wrong guy, wrong time, wrong motives, wrong, wrong, wrong in countless ways. So why should I test once again a door that seemed to be closed to me? Maybe I was just born with bad relationship karma, or had developed an entrenched habit of poor choices; either way, why set myself up to be hurt again – to fail again?

Disregarding my skepticism, I set about the task Gwen had suggested by making a list in three columns. The first was of all the things I wanted in a man – my must haves, the second column contained all the things I absolutely could *not* live with, and the third was for all the things

I'd *prefer* him not to be/do but *could* live with. It was an interesting exercise that took me a couple of weeks to produce and refine. By the time it was finished, I realized how much I did want this man to show up in my life, that I'd only been kidding myself thinking I was done with love. Then I put it away and did not look at it again for several months.

"It doesn't interest me what you do for a living.
I want to know what you ache for, and if you dare to
dream of meeting your heart's longing."

—Oriah Mountain Dreamer, *The Invitation*

In the meantime, I worked on another goal. That same summer I had quite inexplicably had an overnight change in focus. I quite literally awoke one morning determined to lose some weight, and I stormed into it with unusual gusto. The pounds came off rather quickly, and a vague "weight" that I had been carrying on my shoulders for a long time seemed to lift with it. I recalled reading somewhere that the amount of "weight" you carry around on your shoulders is often in direct proportion to how long you have to "wait" for related positive events or circumstances to show up in your life. That seemed to hold true.

Maybe it was the weight loss and a newfound sense of self-esteem, or maybe some ongoing spiritual work that began lifting old layers of the past off of me, or maybe it was just timing, but one day in November my reticence around looking for love again seemed to disappear into thin air. I received an unsolicited e-mail from the online dating website, e-harmony, which lured me in out of curiosity, and before I knew it I was answering questions and filling out the profile – *in search of love*. I rationalized that if I never made any attempt to try this one more time, I would always wonder if I'd missed some "last chance" to correct a long-standing, unhappy pattern.

It is my practice at each New Moon to make some wishes regarding my life in alignment with the energies of that moon.[1] November and

---

[1] See *New Moon Astrology* by Jan Spiller.

December's wishes both included some positive requests regarding this wonderful man I had finally decided I wanted to meet. At some point, in a prayerful meditation, I remember saying, "I do want this, but I don't want the same old thing all over again, so if You can't send me someone of quality, don't send me anyone at all." I truly meant it; it was probably the clearest prayer I've ever uttered, and it was heard. I knew that the moment I met Ken.

Little did I know that just five miles away, after two marriages gone wrong, five kids, and a successful career, Ken had received the same e-harmony email. With similar issues and questions, he too found himself signing up, with a reticence feeling much like my own. He had written to a few women, had met some too, but no one stood out; there had been no sparks.

Back at my house, I was doing the same. The website had put each of us in each other's group, and I had read his info and seen his picture a couple of times. There was something that kept drawing me back, though I held off. I had contacted others first, just as he had. I truly don't remember who contacted who first – I think it was me, but no matter. Once we connected, the rest of the searching just stopped. I entered some kind of altered state for a time, and everything . . . slowed . . . way . . . down. He had my full attention.

I recall those initial emails sent through e-harmony with a warmth that brings such joy to me even now. We slowly released different tiers of information to each other and began the process of more direct communication through which we could ask each other questions about the information we received. In late December he suggested we share our actual e-mail addresses and get out of the awkward set-up on e-harmony, allowing us to have more flowing conversations, not limited as they were on the site. It was during that time that I first began to fall in love with him – or at least into some sort of infatuation. He was warm and engaging, thought provoking, and very open with a hint of flirtatiousness. And all of that made him very sexy! Who knew that at age sixty I could feel that way again?

On New Year's Day 2008 there was a snowstorm of somewhat epic proportions. Everyone was pretty much snowed in, and I was enjoying a good book near the fire and the company of my cats. At some point that morning, I checked my computer, and there was an email from Ken. We wrote back and forth to each other all day, each waiting impatiently for the other's reply.

"Your heart and my heart are very, very old friends."
—Hafiz

They were fun and flirtatious messages, and that evening he sent one that said, "You know, this has been fun, but I didn't join e-harmony to find a pen-pal! Why don't we meet for coffee or dinner sometime soon?" My response was swift and positive. He indicated that he wanted me to be comfortable and so insisted I pick the time and spot, so on January 4, 2008, we met for dinner at a little Thai place near my house at 6pm.

I happened to get there first and was seated in a booth near a window where I could see the door. Pretty soon this tall, slim man in a long black coat walked in and began looking around. He turned in my direction and smiled with an honesty and warmth that I could literally feel across the room. My heart began to pound (audibly, I was certain) and something in me nearly gasped out loud in recognition. At that moment my whole being went soft and quiet and, heart in my throat, I heard myself whisper inside, "Ohhh . . . finally. . . it's You!"

Ken and I talked nonstop through dinner, totally losing track of time, and ended up almost literally being swept out the door by the wait staff well after the restaurant closed at 9:00.

Life would never be the same again.

Getting To Know You

Ken was a member of Measure 4 Measure, a men's chorus, and he loved it. There was a concert scheduled for the Sunday evening right after we met, and he invited me to attend. Giddy new love notwithstanding, it had all been a bit overwhelming, and given my romantic history, I knew that I needed to keep some reasonable space for myself. My feelings for him were so strong, so early on; frankly it kind of scared me. I declined as kindly as I could, promising to go to the next one and citing a busy week, using the cats as an excuse as well and needing to give them some attention.

The morning of the concert, I had an email from Ken, and I was just answering it late that afternoon when he called and we chatted for a little while. His email referenced my curling up with the cats and how he would be thinking about that as he sang, maybe even channeling himself through one of them. When we hung up, even though we had just spoken, I couldn't resist responding to the email in the hope he would see it before he left. The following emails ensued:

Gloria to Ken:

Interesting how seeing someone's email address listed in your mailbox can make the day start out a little better. I haven't had a chance to answer until now but I did notice a smile on my face a couple of times just thinking about cuddling with you and the kitties tonight.

. . . just got off the phone with you and it was nice that you called just now. I'm about to get officially snuggled in with Raven and Angel so it seemed appropriate that you joined in just when you did. I feel like I have lots to share with you and yet little to say in this moment, just feeling very comfy, cozy, and quiet. I'm off to the kitchen to get us all a little bite to eat . . . then hug them both and listen to their purrs as we snuggle in for the evening . . . waiting to see if I can figure out which one of them is you . . . Have a good concert. Talk to you tomorrow. purrrrrrrrrrrrrrrrrrrrrrrr, Gloria

He didn't get my message until he got home later that night. I barely had my coffee in hand the next morning when I hurried to my computer to see if he had responded; this is what awaited me:

Ken to Gloria:

I am speechless!! How in God's name do you think I am going to be able to go to sleep with a message like that? However, if I am going to be awake it would be hard to find a better reason . . . This sure seems like a budding relationship to me. Your line about having a

*lot to share but not many words at the moment fits for
me too. Sleep well. Talk tomorrow. Ken*

I can't begin to explain the grin that came to my face, not to mention the
butterflies in my stomach. Whatever fears I had felt that precipitated
wanting to keep my distance from him melted with this response. I had
flirted unashamedly, and he had flirted right back. I never doubted the
magnetism between us again.

---

*"It doesn't interest me what planets are squaring your
moon. I want to know if you have touched the center
of your own sorrow, . . . I want to know if you can sit
with pain, mine or your own, without moving to hide
it, or fade it, or fix it."*

—Oriah Mountain Dreamer, *The Invitation*

Quickly putting any hesitation behind us, Ken and I launched into a
committed, intentional, deep-sharing stage. He would come over after
work on Tuesdays and we would have a light meal and sit on the couch
all evening, sharing whatever came up in the moment. We called these
our Tuesday Tea Times. It was not simply the wound-sharing stage
that many new couples go through, but an honest acknowledgement
of where we had each gone wrong in the past, where we wanted to do
better in the future.

We had each independently thought at the very onset of our relationship
that if this one didn't work, we were done trying and would live out our
days in singlehood. It was to be the foundation for our new life together,
and we were both clear that something had to change from the ways
each of us had done relationships before. Early on, Ken mentioned a
quote (he loved quotes, so you will find a lot of them within these pages)
about the definition of insanity being to continue doing the same thing
over and over again and expecting a different result. That resonated for
both of us and so became more or less our mission statement.

During one of these conversations we talked about our physical lives. I shared about my high blood pressure and cholesterol and weight issues, and he opened up about his greatest health challenge: he'd had kidney cancer. One kidney had been removed. He said that his doctors were confident they had gotten it all, and he had been symptom-free for quite some time now. We quickly moved on to other more pleasing topics, and I never gave it another thought.

We soon discovered that we each had an affinity for describing our typical thinking process using an appliance metaphor. His, a noisy processor, needed to talk stuff out, and often in some detail, before coming to conclusions. Mine, more of a coffee pot, required things to sit inside and percolate, brew, if you will, before pouring out. These metaphorical descriptors afforded each of us some very early and helpful insights into what would become our communication style that served us well in future situations, paving the way to better understanding in the end.

I had never shared as deeply and openly with another man before Ken. He was so genuine and so easy to talk to, and I just trusted him so implicitly and immediately. I never felt any judgment nor saw so much as a raised eyebrow at anything I ever confided in him about. It was nonetheless difficult for me at times, as I was so afraid I'd scare him off somehow if I was too forthcoming. I feared saying something that was not well thought out, that poorly chosen words would offend or be misconstrued. He struggled some with that as well, so as we returned again and again to our mantra, that we would no longer do things the way we'd done them in previous relationships, we knew we had to find a way to bypass a habit we had both formed.

After dancing around some issues, we finally landed on the answer: to "just blurt" and sort out the verbiage later. Some simple phrasing became the lead in. "Honey, I need to blurt, OK?" "OK. Sweetheart, I'm listening." The "blurter" was letting the "blurtee" know that he or she was about to hear something that might have to go through translation. Therefore, the blurtee would put ego aside and just listen and sort out the meaning afterwards if necessary. It was a way to let either of us express what was bothering us without fear of an overreaction or misunderstanding. The blurter was making it known that they were not sure *how* to say something and in no way wanted to hurt the blurtee. The blurtee was in effect saying that he or she would not take anything personally but would listen with an open heart, and continue with whatever dialogue ensued in order to find clarity for both. The approach worked! I t took a lot of pressure off when t he inevitable wound-sharing sessions came up or when discussions occurred during which we were on opposite sides.

Case in point: In the beginning, of course, extensive cuddling before sleep was soooo important to both of us. Eventually, however, I started to feel a little claustrophobic trying to fall asleep all tangled up with each other. I had spent many years by myself and, at bedtime, liked my space, liked to sprawl a bit and shuffle around. I didn't know how to tell him because it seemed clear that spooning ourselves into sleep was something he really enjoyed. Finally, with the blurt technique, I managed to say it, quite awkwardly and not as graciously as I might have liked. He wasn't thrilled at first, but once I managed to tell him that I did indeed still want to cuddle, I just needed to slip into my own space when it was time to sleep, it all worked out. After that, we cuddled on his side and when it was time, I slid over and we both got what we needed. Sounds simple enough, but it was a milestone for me to be able to be truthful about what I needed and have a way to feel safe expressing it. And surprisingly, once that hurdle was cleared, I found I didn't mind so much anymore when we spooned on *my side* sometimes.

On the first night that Ken slept over he had an interesting experience with one of my feline housemates. He had met Raven, of course, as she would always wander in and say hello, especially when we were having dinner. I'm not sure if she was just looking for a handout, or if she knew we would be settled there for a while and determined that Ken was therefore a captive audience, but she always chose that time to come and rub and purr and seek his touch. Ken apparently always acknowledged her presence with the appropriate demeanor, as she consistently returned with ever-increasing demands for his attention. Though Raven was the far more social of the two, this was a seriously high approval rating from her.

Angel, on the other hand, always my shy girl, did not respond in kind. This is a kitty that was in my life for sixteen years, seven years at the time I met Ken, and some of my friends who visited regularly had never even seen her. She was often referred to as a figment of my imagination! Angel had made appearances, however, for Ken. As we ate, she would stand in the doorway to the hallway (always keep an escape route close by) and watch. We would each say hello and encourage her to come closer. She preferred to just observe, but even that was far more than she gave most people in my life.

The first night that Ken stayed over, the cats could both sense that something was different as I went through the bedtime ritual of feeding them and readying them for my disappearance into sleep. Their quizzical faces kept searching mine for an answer as to why this guy hadn't gone home yet! I patiently explained that he would indeed be staying with us, but clearly they were not convinced of my words. Raven soon got over it and climbed all over us as we chatted together in the dark. Angel apparently opted to think things over on her own and disappeared.

The next morning, Ken got up and went to the kitchen to get us each a mug of coffee. I heard him in the hallway talking "kitty-talk," and I assumed Raven had waylaid him into some rubs on his trek down the hall. When he returned, steaming coffee in hand, I said something about the kitty encounter, asking how Raven was doing today. He replied with a grin, and quite proud of himself, that it hadn't been Raven but Angel who had greeted him. She had patiently waited for him to stop, kneel down (as one should to a princess), and offer his hand. She then allowed him to touch her, stroke her and rub her head, as though she had known him all her life. That was the final stamp of approval: he had to be "the one" if Angel had offered herself to his touch, the ultimate acceptance in her book.

One of the questions in the e-harmony questionnaire asked about our favorite books and what we were currently reading. I had answered that my current book was *What We Ache For* by Oriah Mountain Dreamer. We hadn't spoken about it at the time but one day, Ken asked me more about it, and I gave a brief description of the premise. He was quite curious to know more about her writing, so I brought my CD of Oriah's book *The Invitation* to listen to on a short day-trip we took. He was very taken by it, as I had been. The poem was so meaningful to both of us as it described pretty much how we both felt about the kind of relationship we had each always wanted to have, the kind of relationship we felt we were finding in each other. It was to lead to a special announcement we sent out the following March when we were planning "the merger." I know. Groan. But having both worked in corporate America – the same company actually – we had naturally fallen into this corporate jargon once we started planning on moving in together. It was of great amusement to us, if to no one else.

Ken's sense of humor is legendary and I saw even in the early days of our courtship just how well he used it. One Tuesday evening in March, I casually asked him what had made him decide to join e-harmony. "Well," he said, "sometime last fall, a guy I know abruptly asked me, 'So how's your sex life?'" Ken told me that the question had left him speechless. He later gave the question some consideration, and when the unsolicited e-harmony email showed up in his in-box, he decided to fill it out. Looking me directly in the eyes and giving me his most lecherous and charming grin, he said, "So I did it 'cuz I wanted to have something to tell him if he asked again!" Once the laughter died down, he gave me a more serious answer, but I rather liked the first one just fine. It was so Ken.

Looking back on 2008, it was likely the busiest year of my life and certainly the best, by far. The year was rich with promise and full of the getting-to-know-you experience, the first blush of love, the ga-ga state of adoring each other, the deepening of everything we felt at a gut level before we ever really knew anything about each other. Unaware of our reasons, we were packing everything in that we could, as fast as we could, like there was no tomorrow. I wanted to drink him in as fully as possible and every time I saw him or talked with him that feeling was pervasive.

Less than a week after we met, he was at my house meeting all of my Gateways Sisters[2] at a gathering we were sponsoring. One month into our new circumstances, he asked me to travel with him to Pennsylvania for a work-related trip and to meet one of his best friends, Jim. Just a week later, Gwen came in for a workshop, and Ken met the whole crew. A picture of us taken then is still my favorite photograph of the two of us, obviously crazy about each other and so very happy.

Unknown to me at the time, I would need to pass muster with a small group of his friends who had seen him through a bad divorce and were going to make sure any woman who had her eyes on Ken would have to

---

[2] Gateways was a nonprofit, spiritually-oriented group organized by several ladies within Gwen's Heartseek Gatherings to honor her teachings and provide workshops and retreats on numerous spiritual topics. We all became good friends, sisters of the heart, and still meet under that name in a circle of friendship and love to share our life experiences.

go through them to get there. A charity event that we were attending set me up to meet these friends. I didn't know I was under scrutiny and in retrospect was glad for that; I was nervous enough as it was. We arrived and found our table and went through the motions of meeting and chatting with these wonderful people, all very kind and welcoming that night, but keeping their secret intentions well hidden. I found out only after we got home that I had been the additional agenda and that I'd apparently passed the test.

One of the most important introductions was meeting Ken's two grown children who still lived with him, Stephanie and John. Nervous much? I had butterflies for days before our scheduled dinner together. As near as I could tell it went pretty well. I found I had some immediate rapport with John when we discovered we both liked dragons. Stephanie and I found a comfort zone with girl talk, lost on the men. After the brief but seemingly positive encounter, we all moved about our lives and, soon, I was spending Friday nights and Sunday afternoons with Ken at their house, affording me the chance to see him in his own element and to begin to form a relationship with Stephanie and John.

Another road trip in early summer took us to Columbus, Ohio, to meet Ken's son, Brian, wife Jenn, and their two boys, Alex and Sam. It was a lovely time, and it was immediately clear to me that Brian was Ken's son as they had very much the same sense of humor. Soon after that trip, Ken and I went to Illinois to meet his sisters Jean and Ary and attend a family reunion.

Along the way, Ken met my Aunt Maxine (she loved him immediately) when he pitched in to help her move into her new assisted living apartment and celebrate her 90th birthday. He also met some of my cousins and friends who came to the event. Next, another of his best friends, Mike, met us in the Cumberlands of Kentucky where we spent a weekend getting to know each other, and later we went to Palm Springs and Sedona to meet some of his friends and some of mine. It was pretty much a whirlwind of travel and new people for most of the year.

In the fall, for his birthday, I reserved a B&B for the weekend. It was out in the country in southwestern Michigan where we enjoyed a small one-room cabin of our own. It had a fire pit for the evenings and trails all over the property to walk and enjoy the autumn color. He enjoyed it so much because we had been on the go all year and he appreciated the time away, the quiet, and the slower pace. It was a much needed break for both of us where we could mirror our early days of quiet conversation and connection.

In short, we spent the year meeting each other's people, everyone who was dear to us. We traveled far and wide with day trips and long trips; we touched all the bases we possibly could. It was dizzying as I think about it now, intense and focused, intuitively assimilating all we could, not knowing our time was short, packing a lifetime into a thimble.

"I'm so happy
it's indecent.

If I had won the lottery
  or if assorted fantasies were true, . . .
but there is no excuse for what I feel.

. . . in all these waves of happiness
It's hard to keep my footing."

— Gwenana, from "Wave of Joy" in *Sticks and Stones*
  and Strawberries

Phone calls at 10 p.m.

During the months prior to Ken moving in with me, we developed a lovely routine on the nights we did not spend together at one of our houses. He would always call at 10 p.m., and we'd chat quietly about our day and what was on the agenda for tomorrow. These were unimportant conversations on the surface but they made me feel so very special, and they connected us in ways that actually seeing each other didn't. Looking at it now, I would say that we were made truly inseparable by those calls. It wasn't the giddy, teenage, "oohhh, he called me tonight!" routine. It was, "Oh, our lives are joined now." Now we include each other in our whole life, in our daily ups and downs, not just the excitement of new love.

That insight would eventually lead to many other conversations about "oneness" and "twoness," as I've mentioned previously. The oneness and twoness of our couple-hood often reminded me of my childhood, lying in the dark in my bed, listening to my mom and dad talking quietly in their room down the hall. It always felt so comforting to hear them, even though I couldn't make out exactly what they were saying. And now, how comforting it was to have this man talking quietly to me at night, full circle somehow, and a precious ending to every single day.

How can a simple phone call feel so romantic? I can't explain it, but once we moved in together I really missed the phone call, and I happened to mention it to him one day. One evening, a few days later, he slipped out of bed about 10 p.m. and I assumed he was getting a drink of water or something as he headed for the kitchen. A few seconds slipped quietly by when my phone rang and when I answered, it was Ken. He was calling me from his cell phone out in the kitchen. Ahhhh. We talked on the phone for a long time that night, with me giggling like a teenager because, "Ooooh, he called me!"

Christmas Lights

One day in early spring, Ken s helping me put some things away in the garage, including my outdoor Christmas lights. I wanted some nails put in so I could just hang them during the off months and not have to deal with the tangled web of wire when it was time to put them up again. I was busy with something else as he was putting in the long nails on one side of the garage. When I turned and saw where he put them I nearly laughed out loud. They were so high that I'd have to get up on a ladder to get them off their perch. Walking over to his 6-foot-3-inch frame, I slid my arms around his waist and mentioned this little point to him, to which he just grinned and said, "Let's just assume I'll be here to help you with that, okay?"

Building the Closet

During some conversations that first spring, Ken indicated that he'd be happy to help me do some things around the house if I needed anything. I told him I'd always thought there could be more closet space in this house. He said, "Let's do it," and we began building a rather large closet in one corner of my finished basement. I gave him an idea of what I wanted: shelves to holds bins, space for hanging short and long clothing, and a top shelf for extra bedding and the like. He came up with a design and measured everything. I bought the lumber and the stain, and we set about the project.

Ken did the measuring and cutting, and I took pieces to the garage and did the sanding and staining. Once accomplished, it was pieced together, adjusted, and set into place. All in all, it was a smooth process, taking only a couple of weekends to finish. As we stood and looked it over with satisfaction, he remarked that he thought we should celebrate this milestone over a nice dinner out.

"What milestone?" I asked.

"Well," he said thoughtfully with his famous grin, "I figure if we could do this project together successfully without ending up in a fight, then I'm sure this relationship is good for the long haul! Let's celebrate!"

Cleaning My Car

Another weekend was approaching. As was our usual habit, I stayed at Ken's house on Friday nights, and he stayed at mine on Saturdays. During the day on Saturday we went our separate ways to do whatever needed doing in each camp. That Saturday morning he suggested he take me home and keep my car. He was going to wash and clean the interior of his and he would like to do mine as well if I didn't need it that day. I didn't, and he picked me up later in my now sparkling clean, well vacuumed and manicured vehicle.

I'd never had a man take care of me quite the way Ken did and this is only one example of many thoughtful things Ken did for me "just because." There is no punch line here, no funny commentary or witty repartee. He was simply the most caring and generous man I have ever met, always giving of his time and energy to do something special for me.

Illinois versus Michigan

Stephanie, Ken's daughter, got us tickets to the 2008 Illinois–Michigan football game for Ken's birthday. His alma mater was Illinois, so of course he was a die-hard Illinois fan, though the record of their wins over Michigan was not the best. His son John dropped us off at the stadium, and through the chaos of thousands of bodies milling about, we finally found our seats. It was a fairly typical fall day, a bit chilly but sunny, and we were in good spirits. Ken wore his Illini attire. Having none myself, I wore the associated attire of my alma mater, Alma College. We ended up seated amongst a primarily Michigan crowd. It was an exciting game with Michigan pulling out in front early on, but Illinois showed some spunk and scored some too. As the game progressed, Illinois began to take control, and every time they scored or pulled off a great play, the meager numbers of Illinois fans screamed and yelled in joy, as did we. Luckily the Michigan fans around us were good natured, and when it was all over, Illinois had won, something like 48 to 20 I think. Ken was jubilant. I had never seen him so happy, and I was so happy for him. I don't believe I've ever been so happy for someone else, and we basked in the joyous aura that surrounded us for days.

Golf as Passion

Oh my, how Ken loved golf! He played with the guys, he played with business associates, and it didn't take him long to lure me back into it. I had played for a few years some twenty years before, and I thought I was done with it, but playing with Ken made me love it again, not only because I loved him and wanted to share this sport with him, but because he made it so easy to do so. I'd played various games and sports with other men in my life, including golf. It was rarely enjoyable, because they always became so competitive that it ruined the fun for me. Ken was helpful, but not too helpful. He was never the type to butt in and give me pointers or comment on my game unless I asked. He helped where he could, and otherwise just let me play, encouraging me and cheering me on when I was really on my game, and being supportive when I was not. As a result, we got on very well together on the golf course, as we did just about anywhere, and we were tickled that we'd found something we could look forward to sharing on into our future.

The Dragonlady

At the point when I met Ken, I had been working out with a personal trainer. Josh had some intricate and wondrous tattoos, and the artwork and the idea of having a tattoo intrigued me. Around my birthday, March of 2008, I had received my usual yearly astrology reading. My astrologer had commented on something in my chart alluding to major new starts and suggested I consider some wild and crazy act to cement this time period into my consciousness. I doubt a tattoo was what he had in mind, but I responded completely to the idea and immediately inquired about the guy who did Josh's tats.

Josh set up an appointment for me. What else could I do but have a dragon placed on my shoulder to protect and carry me into the soaring flight of this new relationship with Ken? (Mind you, we were barely ten weeks in at this point.)

I decided not to tell Ken in advance. With some trepidation, I showed it to him that evening, explaining the whys and so forth. Without skipping a beat, he met my dragon tattoo with happy surprise. He was totally geeked about it. "I can't wait to tell people my girlfriend has a tattoo!" he said. "And she drives a stick shift!" We shared easy laughter at his reaction, and I thought he should also get a tattoo – an otter of course, but he never did.

I soon came to see that there would always be laughter, support, and acceptance, from this extraordinary, dear man. Not quite three months into the relationship at that point and I already couldn't imagine life without his smile.

Special Gifts

By the time we arrived at Christmas 2008, I was full of all the joy and wonder of a five-year-old at the holidays. We spent an evening decorating my tree, starting a new tradition for entering this season of Peace and Love. We baked Christmas cookies at his house, and Stephanie and John pitched in to help. We sent some Christmas cards out together to our mutual friends and family.

And then, of course, we came to gift-giving. It all came together smoothly. We spent an afternoon/evening at his house where we exchanged with his kids, and then we had Christmas Eve with just the two of us at my house. We shared a lovely dinner and then set about the presents. We had earlier talked about gifts, and budgets, and wanting the presents to be meaningful in some way, as well as fun.

I chose, for the most part, all manner of smaller gifts, both comical and sweet, in order to give Ken lots of things to unwrap. My intention and message was "gifts in extraordinary abundance," that represented not only gratitude for all that he had given me through the year but all the goodness and plentitude I wished for him, resplendent reciprocity. There was a wind chime clock, a joke because I complained that his alarm clock was too loud, some aftershave duly named "King," and several other items that had to do with some quirks and traits that I'd uncovered during our first year together. Saving a special, gift for last,

I had him unwrap a set of Runes I made for him, along with his own copy of the corresponding book.[3]

We had often used my set during the previous year, Runes that I had received, handmade, from Gwen. It is an oracle that I had loved using for years and once I began sharing it with him, Ken also appreciated the messages very much and always found that they resonated with him as insightful and thought provoking. This was my gift to him of Spirit and of Love. I'd included a personal note about their meaning, and as he read it, it felt like something sacred had bound us together.

Ken's gift to me was so marvelously romantic and thoughtful. Three packages were presented. I was to open them all and then figure out the message they carried. The first was a gift card for Great Harvest Breads, a local bakery offering both practical and decadent breads, cookies, muffins, and other delectable goodies. The second was a bottle of my favorite red wine. "Okay," I was thinking, "where is this leading?" Ken is grinning at me as I try to figure out the message. Then I opened the final package to find *The Call*, the second book of Oriah's trilogy (after *The Invitation*). It took me only a few seconds to see it, "Oh", I cooed, "a loaf of bread, a jug of wine, and thou beside me!" The book came with his intention that we read it together, a chapter every Friday night (still considered our date night), allowing Oriah's beautifully worded thoughts to wrap us in a warm cocoon together, holding hands.

There is nowhere to go . . .

There is no waiting for something to happen,
no point in the future to get to.
All you have ever longed for is here in this moment, right now.

—Oriah Mountain Dreamer, *The Call*

---

[3] Runes are a set of 25 stones, each marked with one of 25 glyphs as rendered in The Book of Runes by Ralph Blum. It is a form of an ancient oracle meant to "provide a mirror for the magic of our Knowing Selves." The book offers interpretations of these glyphs that can speak to you of change and growth, not of fortune telling, but of your own inner seeker of truth and a guide to the subconscious.

4

Reflection

Yearn forward
with a heart that calls to memories
that hang on stars beyond the reach of words.

The force of yearning
pulls the dreamer toward the dream
and breathes the heart's desire into life.

Coming out of the dream of that wonderful Christmas, I found myself again in my living room on a gloomy day in November 2009 . . . alone.

I had been briefly transported into a blissful, golden scene but now found myself still here, in a state of gray. Returned to a present that shattered my heart yet again, I experienced the memory of the bitter conclusion of that dream. Only a moment ago I was warm in his arms again, laughing and talking, wrapped in the cozy comfort of love. And then the gloom descended once more, mirroring the day outside my window.

Guilt, Regret, and the Angry God

The November following Ken's death was more cold and dreary than any in my memory. In the days and weeks following my discovery of the phone call of October 19, I pleaded with him to come to me in dreams. He did not. I waited and waited; still he did not appear. I wrote incessantly in my journal, mostly about my pain and the unfairness of it all, still angry with God for "taking" him.

I slowly came to an awareness that I had ended up stuck in a very old belief system, of a God of Reward and Punishment, a God of Vengeance. I'd never thought that I'd held onto those childhood beliefs until then.

I recalled being a very little girl, perhaps three or four, in the first church I ever went to, sitting with Mom and Dad in the solid wooden pews on Sunday morning. At some point during the service, the children were sent downstairs for Sunday school, but the first part of the service was attended by the whole family. The minister was apparently a fire-and-brimstone kind of guy, and all I remember was an impression that the congregation was being reprimanded about something I didn't understand. Questions in my little child-mind went unanswered: "What is he so mad about? Why is he yelling so much? Did we do something wrong? Is God mad too?"

"To know that God's maternal hands hold one's life, like a baby. That is so not me, and is really all that I want."

— Anne Lamott, *Help Thanks Wow,*
   The Three Essential Prayers

Somehow, as I was led to Sunday school, where we sang songs like, "Jesus loves the little children" and "Jesus loves me," I must have decided that Jesus was kind and loving, while God was a scary tyrant to be feared.

Now, at age sixty-two, the whole belief system I had built over the last twenty years suddenly imploded, leaving only that three-year-old's picture of God. My open, loving, creative, eclectic spiritual practice was all gone, and I had nothing left to lean on. If God was indeed this vengeful being, then everything else I thought I'd come to believe was wrong.

That was proven to me by the fact that Ken was gone, had been *taken away*. Before Ken, I had come to believe that "why?" was a question better left unasked, that "why" is not for us to know, and that trust in The One who does know is paramount. Now, with this old God reemerging in my consciousness, "Why?" was the only question I could ask. And the only answer I could think of was that I had done something *very wrong* and God had taken Ken as punishment. I had come to believe in these last few years that God wants our happiness and now He had betrayed my trust in that. So which God was the true God? Certainly it had to be the God of my childhood.

I wrote like I was possessed, going over and over everything I could remember during the time Ken and I were together. All my supposed shortcomings landed on the page like fingers pointing at me in accusation: I had retreated into an old habit of losing focus on my own life, my own path, to immerse myself with a man; I had dropped out because of a man, often bailing on Gateways and my friends. I had failed to stay on track and on purpose in my own life; and perhaps most of all, I had failed Ken by forgetting our mantra and not doing things differently this time.

All of my regrets when Ken was ill came back to haunt me. Questions arose about his care. Did I do all I could have? Did I hold him enough? Did I take his hand enough? Say I love you enough? Had we even talked about his feelings, about what was happening to him, his fears, his needs? Had I asked if he had any wishes in particular about his passing and after? Unbelievably, I could not remember! Did we say all we needed to say during those last weeks and days, or had I put a wall between us (as I had done so many other times in my life) so I could stay in denial?

I decided I had failed miserably – again, and so Ken, my perceived reward at this end of life, had been taken away as punishment for my repeated failures. It seemed logical; it was my own fault that he was gone. If I had just been better, if I'd been "a good girl," if I had just "done the right thing," he would still be alive. The pit I was digging for myself was getting deeper, and it had barely been six weeks since Ken had passed.

December 2009 soon arrived with all of its laughter and songs and messages of love. I felt none of it. Mostly, it sickened me. The days wore on, and I managed to navigate the holidays by putting on the face I thought people would be more comfortable with. Besides, I didn't want to see the pity on their faces. Angry and sullen underneath the mask I wore, I found a somber resoluteness that held me together. There was no joy, no future, no God that I could accept. I had fully entered The Void.

When 2009 finally came to an end, I couldn't have been more pleased to see it go.

Nonetheless, I looked into the New Year with no additional improvement in either my mood or my attitude. My journal entries continued in angry bursts and sorrowful wallowing. I found no comfort in anything that had previously supported me spiritually. The loss was so painful I hadn't even contacted Gwen, and I sat in a self-imposed isolation relishing my anger and my resentment of this "God" that had so betrayed me. However, while I thought I had broken ties with all things spiritual, I was to find that, as they say, "old habits die hard". I had for many years performed a ritual at the New Year, where I spent some time reviewing the year just past, looking for some reconciliation of events therein, and through use of dreams, oracles, and journaling, took a glance forward to what I might expect or intention for the future.

While the future in general seemed to hold nothing, the past was certainly replete with unresolved emotions, and I felt compelled to look at it as a means to help make some sense of what had befallen me . . . befallen us. In *What We Ache For*, Oriah Mountain Dreamer alludes to the patterns and connections that lead us to meaning in our lives and to Victor Frankl (survivor of the Nazi concentration camps who wrote *Man's Search for Meaning*). She said that *"he urged us not to ask what the events of our lives mean but to take responsibility for creating meaning from the events of our lives."* I was about to undertake that very journey.

In the early days of 2010, I fell into an intense review of 2009, putting the pieces of the year together with fragments of memories, trying to find some peace, some answers, some escape from the pain that gripped me. It had been a year of events and emotions I'd never had time to process; a continuum of highs and lows, never seeing the train coming until it hit. I was yearning for some resolution to my despair, and this sojourn was my only hope. If, as I believed, there was no future, then all I had was the past. So I needed to explore it. How and why had Love gone so wrong – again?

On January 4, 2010, I found myself staring out my front window at the birds devouring the seed I'd just put in the feeder earlier that morning. Just two years ago to the day I had been giddily preparing for my first date with Ken. In truth, I was already in love with him. O ur e mail correspondences had shown me the man I had longed for my entire life, and when he walked in the door that first night I knew he was "the one." My heart had opened instantly, instinctively, and there was no reason to look back. That soaring bliss had plunged into a despair of equal measure and it just wasn't fair. My rambling mind responds – "but life isn't fair" – and my stomach turns at the phrase.

I settled into my retreat and began to reconstruct the worst year of my life. My resistance was strong, as I wanted to avoid the pain. But soon, a 2009 that was as tragic as 2008 had been perfect began to emerge, and I journaled non-stop for days.

The Beginning of The End

2009 had begun much the same as 2008 had. We took a trip to Florida for Ken's annual golf outing with some business acquaintances who had met at that time of year for some time now to network and enjoy the game together. After that, we visited some good friends of Ken's whom I hadn't yet met. During the trip, Ken began to complain of some aches in his right shoulder. He thought it was the golf, having not swung a club in several months. We didn't give it much thought and enjoyed our time with his friends before returning home.

February brought us to our second Valentine's D ay together. I had a romantic notion that he sweetly complied with: we made each other a CD playlist of songs that formed a sort of love letter, each to the other. How wondrous it had been to share this music from our hearts and know we would always have that as a memory of this stage when the romance was still so alive and strong. I fixed us a special meal with scallops (his favorite) and chocolate at the end (for me). Ken also brought home a fun book about keeping the romance in a relationship. It was full of different things to do for and with each other, with the suggestion to pick something in secret and surprise the other with it periodically, but not routinely – the unexpected element being an important part of "romantic." I was touched that he recognized my need for romance and had put his customary thoughtfulness into the idea.

One stormy winter night in front of the fireplace we began musing about what it might be like to live together and what this "merger" might look like. Though we were both assuming Ken would move in with me, we were considering the possibility of buying a home together to start fresh with a new space that was neither his nor mine, but ours. Timing was also a question. Stephanie was seeing Kevin at that time; they had started dating only about six weeks or so before Ken and I met. Ken felt that they might move in together soon as well, and John was thinking about moving in with two buddies, so the timing seemed right for us to name a date in hopes of setting it all in motion. We decided on May 1: May Day, Beltane, spring, new beginnings.

To that end, we soon found ourselves in a delightful conversation about how to announce this to our friends and family. Without question, we both wanted it to be a rather formal announcement. Wanting to take our time on the question of marriage, it seemed even more appropriate. Since I had introduced Ken to Oriah Mountain Dreamer and her poem and book *The Invitation*, it had come to epitomize for both of us the story of our relationship. Over the course of a few days we worked on an official announcement of our new living arrangements, using some of Oriah's words and our own to express our intentions and our union.

Just before we were to mail out the announcements, Ken surprised me with the idea that we should get rings. He wanted there to be rings to symbolize our commitment. We'd had some discussions earlier, as our 40 relationship had deepened about marriage in general. Both of us felt unsure of our need for marriage; we both felt secure enough to be together, to trust it all, without marriage. But now Ken said he felt rings would be not only a symbol of our love and commitment to each other, but of this new beginning for both of us, together. With his ever-insightful ability to ask the right question at the right time, he said, "I know in the past we trusted what we had enough to forego marriage; do we trust it enough now to make exchanging rings a tangible component of our next step?"

I couldn't have loved him more in that moment. I melted like butter in the warmth of his smile. Yes. Rings. We spent some time at the local mall that week and emerged with our rings, eager to wear them and share the event with loved ones. Engaging in a quiet little ceremony of our own while sitting on his bed one evening after dinner, we placed a ring on each other's finger, grinning and giggling like we were just kids and had never done this before. Indeed it all truly felt so new.

Universe continued to conspire to send us more joy. My aunt had a time-share in Florida that I had used on a few occasions. After showing her our rings, she offered it to us as a sort of "honeymoon gift." My birthday fell during that week, so we thought it would be a great way to celebrate. It would be our second trip to Florida in three months, but why not?

In the course of planning the trip, we decided to make it a bit of a family outing. We had not yet spent much time with Ken's son Brian, wife Jenn, and Alex and Sam, so we invited them along. It would be a nice vacation for all of us.

A LOVE STORY

It was a lovely week. We overlooked a small harbor on the gulf side where we enjoyed our morning coffee or evening glass of wine on the balcony while watching the fishing boats, leisure boats, and tourist boats busily going about their day. We saw pelicans catching fish, wading birds carefully stalking the shoreline, dolphins leaping out of the water, and all the other tourists milling about below. There was always a lot of activity, things to see and do. The time-share had its own pool, lots of stores for shopping and browsing, restaurants, and an ice cream shop right below our unit. How could it be anything but fun?

For the most part it was. Usually we all went everywhere together, but Ken and I took the kids to the pool one afternoon so Brian and Jenn could have some time to themselves. Later, they did the same for Ken and me. That day was my birthday, and Ken took me to a seafood restaurant for my favorite – lobster.

The only thing that disrupted our play was Ken's shoulder. It had continued to nag him since the first Florida trip and had begun to get worse. He was taking a lot of Tylenol, and I'd massage his shoulder and neck every night before we went to sleep. But sleep itself had become less than fully restful. He agreed to go see his doctor when we got home.

Ken and I had driven to Florida, and when we left at the end of the week to head north, we planned to spend some time in the Smoky Mountains as we meandered home. We took our time and made our way through the mountains peppered with several stops to enjoy the scenery along our route. We spent the better part of two days in the National Park, checked out all the tourist stops in Cherokee, climbed to lookout points and took short hikes, pausing to look at the breathtaking scenery stretching miles into the foggy distance. True to its name, the visual effect of the fog captured our imaginations. We both remarked that we could feel the spiritual nature of these mountains and mused about how the Native American peoples who once lived here experienced the presence of Spirit and a reverence for this land.

At one point we stopped at an overlook near a narrow river to have lunch and listen to the gurgling waters. There was a stone wall about bench high, and we sat there watching the river flow by. It was a lovely warm day, sunny, blue skies, carrying the smell of spring on the early April breeze. I had my camera with me, and seeing Ken sitting on the wall with such a wondrous background of trees on the riverbank below, I took his picture.

When we got home and I got the pictures developed, I was so disappointed in that p articular photo. Some abnormality in the film, I thought, or somehow light had gotten inside the camera, but whatever happened, there on Ken's right side, a reddish streak started in the sky above him, grazed the right side of his head, and covered over his right shoulder and disappeared into his chest.

At home, Ken's shoulder continued to bother him, and as promised, he decided to go to the doctor and have it checked out. It was also time to have his yearly test, post-kidney surgery, to be sure all was well. That test came back fine, and the x-rays of his shoulder showed nothing either, so he was given a script for physical therapy. The doctor thought it could be a rotator cuff problem or a pulled ligament or tendon.

In the meantime, we were enmeshed in planning the Great Merger. Stephanie and Kevin had made their plans, and John was also moving out. Rather than try to sell my house, buy another, and both of us have to move, Ken and I decided the best plan was for him to move into my house first, and then regroup around our own plans for the future once the kids were settled and we could think clearly. Ken was also ready to sell or dissolve his business and enter some phase of retirement, which seemed to underscore the wisdom of staying put for a while.

As May 1 neared, Ken began packing, and one night, after helping to get some things boxed up, we snuggled up in bed to watch TV. We discussed the details of the move and agreed that everything was going smoothly. Ken gave me a hug and happily blurted out, "This is all just so perfect. I could die now a happy man!"

My reaction was swift and forceful. "Don't *ever* say that!" I was surprised by my outburst, and so was Ken. Trying to soften the intensity, I added, "We're magic Honey; don't invite disaster; you know, things can always get even better!" But the effects of my sudden reaction stayed with me most of the next morning and my heart raced every time I recalled his words.

May 1 arrived. Plans were all laid out for getting the last of the boxes moved for both Stephanie and John, and loads were taken to their respective new homes that morning. In the afternoon, the rest of the items were either coming to my house or going to a donation bin, and soon the dream would become reality. I was beside myself with excitement and joy, knowing that tonight we'd be living together. I moved my furniture into the guest room to make room for Ken's king-sized bedroom set to come in. Other adjustments were made to allow space for his clothes, personal effects, and a few pieces of furniture. My car had been moved to one side to allow his to share the garage. Ken made the last trip back to his house to pack up and deliver the goods that were to be donated. While he was gone, I fitted our bed with a set of new sheets and comforter I had purchased on the sly, as well as a pair of new lamps for the end tables, all as a surprise for Ken. New home. New room. New life. New start.

All was perfect, whole, and complete.

Standing In The Fire

May 23, 2009, was a beautiful, warm, sunny spring afternoon. I was happily engaged in the garden, planting the last of the spring flowers, mostly the sweetly scented alyssum in shades of pinks and purples that would fully line the length of the sidewalk. Ken drove in around 3:30 or 4:00, early for him to be home, I thought. Maybe he'd had enough of the office on such a gorgeous day and decided to come home early to enjoy it. As he walked toward me his smile belied something hidden just below the surface. After a cheery hello, he leaned over and gave me a quick kiss, asked how the planting was going, and told me how good the garden was looking. Then, taking a deep breath, he added, "I have something I need to tell you."

I looked up at him from where I was kneeling on the ground. The sun was in my eyes, and he was backlit so I couldn't read his expression.

He whispered, "The cancer is back."

"What?" I gasped, my heart falling into my stomach.

"It doesn't interest me who you know or how you came to be here. I want to know if you will stand in the center of the fire with me and not shrink back."

—Oriah Mountain Dreamer, *The Invitation*

As I stood up, Ken briefly recounted his conversation with the doctor: the cancer was in his lung this time – on the right side. "But let's not talk about it out here," he said.

Fear gripped me. My mind couldn't make sense of what he was saying. Aside from the shoulder issue he'd been dealing with, he seemed so healthy, energetic, strong. Speechless, I left my garden tools laying in the dirt, and we went inside.

We sat on the sofa, a place of such joy this past year. My mind raced; he had just moved in; we had so many plans; what was going to happen now; what did this mean? Ken gave me the meager details his doctor had shared. It was metastatic – from the previous kidney cancer. They would be deciding on a treatment plan soon.

Cancer sat in our laps like a stone. We barely moved. We just held hands for what seemed like hours, saying little, each gazing helplessly into the other's eyes and our own dark chasms, unable to form the questions or get the answers we both so desperately needed.

In that darkness, as though in some impulsive, knee-jerk response to the stress of "not knowing," Ken said, "C'mon, let's go get some chocolate." We drove to the store and picked up some Snickers (his favorite) and a couple other varieties and returned home. Not surprisingly, there was no solace to be found in the chocolate. Finally, we numbly made our way to bed and held each other into sleep.

"Sit beside me in long moments of shared solitude,
knowing both our absolute aloneness and our undeniable belonging.
Dance with me in the silence and in the sound of small daily words,
holding neither against me at the end of the day."

—Oriah Mountain Dreamer, *The Dance*

By morning, we had each found safety in a denial of our fear. In the following weeks and months, we never dealt with that denial and never spoke of our fears through all that was to come. That would be one of my biggest regrets.

Reality Check

As my two-day 2010 retreat came to a close, I knew I needed to *do* something. Tears streaming down my face, I rose from the nightmare and fought back against the darkness. I couldn't continue to wallow and sink more deeply into the abyss. I had to wake up and somehow find the strength to move beyond this pain. I thought I could just push it all away as I had done with God, but God was pushing back.

Perhaps because I could not yet believe in a future, and the present was still too painful, the only place I could go was the past. During those initial days of 2010 I had cautiously looked back at those early days when Ken and I were brand new, and even before we had actually met, exploring and revisiting that time when life had been bliss and joy was abundant.

Once I had been able to relive "the best of times," I had allowed myself small glimpses of the present and continued to return to my gloomy thoughts and the "worst of times." Slowly, however, my natural instinct to explore returned.

What came into my consciousness during early 2010 was not, at first glimpse, significant beyond the life raft it provided. Later I was to see that 2010 gave me a new foundation, a place from which to look at my situation from another perspective.

I began by allowing myself to be led to next steps – not by mental endeavor, but by letting instinctual movements reign. I found myself drawn to re-reading *The Artist's Way* by Julia Cameron, and I began the daily process of her now famous Morning Pages. Through very nearly the whole year, following this practice daily, I wrote volumes. An intuitive exploration, these pages are intended to bring up what is just under the surface and by stream of consciousness writing it becomes unearthed. As expected, initially much of it was blither. But eventually, as these pages are meant to do, I began to uncover myself from the murky emotions and thinking of my recent past. It was a long, slow, arduous process and continued to be peppered with bouts of anger, grief, and guilt, but, regardless, I felt like I was getting somewhere.

As with my attraction to *The Artist's Way,* numerology resurfaced in my life when I felt the need for a form of simple exploration and inquiry. I had dabbled in it some years before, and one day, out of curiosity, I picked up an old book. It wasn't long before I began to use it again as a way to study all aspects of my life, to try to access answers to the "whys." Was there any larger purpose to the tumultuous events of 2009? It opened up a new door and a sense that behind that door I might find some defining information that might give me a more solid hold on the tenuous balance I had begun to achieve.

First, I did the numerology on our names and birthdates. Numerology on Ken's full name had reduced to an 18/9. My full name, now that we had married, included "King," and adding that to my maiden name, it yielded the mirror image of his, an 81/9. An immediate assessment of all this implied ushered in a new sense of the magic I had felt when we met. Male/female; oneness/twoness; 18 and 81, like a set of bookends – there were countless analogies as my mind bounded in quick succession in a free association flow, and I let the implication of these numbers wash over me. By this simple synchronicity of mirrored numbers, I became convinced I was being shown a path of discovery. I felt an excitement that had been lost to me for a very long time.

Marcel Proust said, "The real voyage of discovery consists not in seeking new landscapes, but in having new eyes." I certainly felt like I had new eyes at this point. This one small discovery had opened me to a new horizon, and the exploration through numerology began in earnest. It was my new "magic," as not only my new name but every nuance of life, when put under that microscope, yielded new insights and messages that I had come to believe had been sent by Ken. Like the telephone call, he was using this to help me take the next steps. I couldn't explain this return to belief in something, for certainly believing he was sending messages implies belief in other things as well, right? I still couldn't feel his presence exactly, nor did he come in dreams for some time, but as the Dark Night began to yield to the softness of that first pale dawn, I had discovered that I still trusted Ken and believed in us, whether there was a God involved or not. This was the foundation upon which I was to rebuild my spiritual beliefs and come back into the light. Ken and I had started out magic, and we still were.

5

The Search

Shake me awake from dreams.
Rattle my bones.
Drum on my soul.
Burn off my doubt.
Spirit of a living God fall fresh on me.

Over the course of 2010, I seemed to always have several books going at once. So, during those first few months of the year, I was not only reading *The Artist's Way* and various numerology books, but I was also re-reading *The Anatomy of The Spirit* by Carolyn Myss. How I came to it has no dramatic story. I had not been looking for something or thinking my way to a next step. As before, I simply gravitated toward it like a magnet, picked it up one day and began to read. Though I would have denied it at the time, God, it seems, was trying to get my attention.

This book explores the 7 Sacraments, the 7 Chakras, and the 7 levels of the Tree of Life in the Kabbalah, as Myss overlays these belief sets onto each other to view their Universal messages. Out of that came my intention to do a series of personal ceremonies to renew and reaffirm myself through my own exploration of the 7 sacraments and chakras. This would be a seven-month-long journey as I sought solid ground and a new spiritual blueprint for my life.

"The inevitable always happens. We need discipline and patience to overcome it. And hope. It isn't a question of placing hope in the future. It is a question of re-creating our own past."

—Paulo Coelho, *The Fifth Mountain*

After the long period of internalizing, I finally got in touch with Gwen, and we began an ongoing discussion about the Myss book as I re-read the chapters. It became the fodder of many of my Morning Pages and consumed my thoughts more and more as I explored through the lens of my loss. It was an arduous process, and with Gwen's guidance I started to unravel various aspects of all that had happened over the last two years and who I had become as a result. She helped me uncover the questions and open to the answers it held for me. With her help, I constructed and immersed myself in a personal, in-depth approach to this process, including a personalized ceremony to mark the end of each sacramental sojourn.

In truth, I doubt that I understood what I was looking for at the time. All I knew was that I was yearning for answers for which I had no questions. This was simply the path that showed the most light. I spent from March through September of 2010 seeking. Following are the 7 chakras and corresponding 7 Sacraments as listed in Carolyn Myss's book:

1st Chakra (Root/Tribal Power):
Sacrament of Baptism

2nd Chakra (Sacral/Power of Relationships):
Sacrament of Communion

3rd Chakra (Solar Plexus/Personal Power):
Sacrament of Confirmation

4th Chakra (Heart/Emotional Power):
Sacrament of Marriage

5th Chakra (Throat/Power of Will):
Sacrament of Confession

6th Chakra (Third Eye/Power of the Mind):
Sacrament of Ordination

7th Chakra (Crown/Spiritual Connector):
Sacrament of Extreme Unction

As I studied, and wrote, and immersed myself more deeply, I found that not every stage was a profound one in terms of my Dark Night. All had their impact certainly, each provided a piece of the puzzle I was constructing, but some clearly brought important insights to the surface more than others.

The First Sacrament: Baptism

One explanation Myss gives for the spiritual adult's baptism speaks of symbolizing "our commitment to acceptance of personal responsibility for living honorably as a member of the human tribe," and through this commitment, honoring our own lives. This appeared to be where I was focused when I started down this path. It felt important to be able to honor my own life in some meaningful way, and I began writing my Morning Pages in search of what that meant.

In reading Myss's interpretation, the first thing that stood out to me was how our "tribal" associations influence everything at all stages of our life. Different tribes have different and varying importance to us at different times and affect how we choose to interpret life. Our first tribe, our family, is responsible for protecting us. This tribe teaches us the ropes within our particular society when we are in a very vulnerable stage of life, making sure we know the rules that keep us safe. This relates to the Sacrament of Baptism in that our parents and family promise to do all this for us, to keep us safe, and to introduce us formally to the rest of the tribe. The First Chakra also relates to tribal power, i.e. traditional beliefs, law and order, basic necessities, safety in numbers, tribal boundaries, loyalty within a tribe, security – learning how to stand, but within the tribe and according to its values.

As I wrote about this concept in my journal, I began to piece together not only the basis for my original belief system with the angry and vengeful God of my childhood, but also the God I had come to know as an adult: Spirit, Universe, Grandfather – the wise and gentle energy I had come to know through the chosen tribes I honored in my later life. With this recognition, I felt I was ready for Ceremony.

I couldn't imagine anyone but Gwen, my Spiritual Mother and Mentor, to baptize me. Gwen had, after all, metaphorically baptized me years ago when I met her and had begun this new spiritual path. And where else but in San Diego, Gwen's home, where the Ocean Mother's song could wash over me, leaving me pure and in innocence for this new life I was about to begin? It had been in San Diego with Gwen, near the seemingly infinite Pacific Ocean, that I had spent so much time in serene contemplation finding my spiritual center and strength. Now, when all that seemed so far away, I yearned for this place of peace to bring me new truths or somehow return me to a place where the old ones still held fast. This ceremony had to happen in San Diego with my beloved Gwendolyn, whose love and wisdom had reached out to me over the telephone line so many times in recent weeks, encouraging this quest.

Gwendolyn

When I met Gwen Jansma in 1993, my life was forever changed. Her teachings and her very Being have had the single most profound spiritual influence on me, and I am so grateful and blessed to have been led to her.

Gwen was an extraordinary woman. I met her through a friend of mine who had been attending her "Heartseek Gatherings" for some time. One day, my friend showed me Gwen's brochure and said she thought I might be interested. I had an immediate, almost visceral, recognition of her work. While it took me another couple of months to actually sign up for one of her Gatherings, it was never far from my thoughts. The subject for that first weekend was "If I Should Wake Before I Die," and although I had studied the few paragraphs that had been sent describing the topic, it was nonetheless not enough for my left brain to comprehend; my right brain was apparently still asleep.

The day came for the Gathering, and I drove to the meeting place, made a wrong turn, and by the time I arrived I was nearly late for the start time. I found a space in the packed parking lot, gathered my stuff, made a dash for the door . . . and walked through the wrong entrance by mistake, or so I thought. It was an area where the food for our lunchtime potluck was to be placed, and a few bowls of crackers and nuts and the like were already scattered about. I noticed a small woman standing there, picking up and munching on a couple of morsels. She was the only one in sight, and she turned to look as she heard me enter. With an easy acknowledgment of my scattered energy, she smiled and slowly said, "Oh, you must be Gloria: we *finally* meet," as though she had been expecting me for years. Gwen took both of my hands in hers and looked into my eyes (a regular habit, I was to find), and held my gaze for a few moments with the kindest, most loving smile I'd ever seen. Then she guided me into the room where all the "fun" was to happen.

A LOVE STORY

I was, in a word, hooked. I spent the next twenty years in every local Gathering save one, and some not so local. There I met so many wonderful people, many of whom are still my friends today. We shared our stories, spent time in meditation and a variety of other unfamiliar "woo-woo" activities that I was totally unprepared for, and I listened with rapt attention to this woman, Gwen, who blew me away with her insights, teachings, and unique spiritual connectedness. Over the years, her words would come back to me at unexpected moments, surprising me by their wit, wisdom, and intuitive knowing, words whose meaning had often been lost on me when she first offered them. They often echo in my memory, shaking loose something previously lost from my consciousness. Her books of poems continue to reveal to me layers of myself which have been in unawareness for years. Her intuitive and psychic skills were always on target and her influence on my life has been epic.

A case in point: Many long years ago, sometime in the mid-1990s, we were in Circle at one of Gwen's Gatherings. As she often did, she was working with everyone individually and had come to me. I recall she was sitting in the chair right next to me, which was rare; I was usually somewhere on the opposite side of the room. This placement seemed to anchor the experience, as I do not remember the context but only a couple of sentences she spoke as she sat there. When she worked with anyone, she would sit or stand directly facing them and utilize that wondrous "eye to eye" connection she did so well. On this particular day, she turned her chair to face mine and we sat there knee to knee as she spoke. To the best of my memory, she said, "Someday in the future you will be communicating or generating some sort of spiritual work through what appears to be an unusual medium. I want to say electronically in some way, but I don't know what that means." Neither did I . . . use of computers as well as all manner of electronic mediums was in its infancy at the time.

In 2014, I spent the entire year writing a blog and planning this book, which I hope to release as an e-book as well as in paperback. I can hear Gwen's laughter ringing in my ears. It now seems very clear what she was referencing that day.

After many years of gatherings in Michigan and trips to her hometown of San Diego, various words and phrases became her trademarks. Many of us who knew Gwen still find these words falling naturally out of our own mouths, carrying her spirit forward by doing so. The following seem to present themselves most often, and her presence seems almost palpable as we quote her routinely in conversations.

"Breathe, just breathe."

"All is well."

"You can't do it wrong."

"All outcomes are the same."

"It is in the silence that Spirit speaks."

"Trust Timing; timing is everything."

"What is once joined in Love can never be broken."

A couple of other practices come forward as those I most associate with Gwen that have meant the most to me personally. One is the use of the Viking Runes. Gwen, living near San Diego, would go to her favorite beach in Del Mar to wander great lengths of it, taking in the nearly unending vistas of ocean and sky. While doing so, she collected all kinds of shells and stones worn smooth and flat by the ocean. She would make sets of Runes with them and then give these sets away at her Gatherings. The set I received from her more than twenty-five years ago is one of my most cherished possessions.

I have made sets on occasion for others, and I always felt a connection with Gwen as I made them. As she did, I collected flat, more or less quarter-sized black stones from Torrey Pines Beach, the one Gwen had always roamed, and brought them back home with me to Michigan. In ceremonial fashion I separated them into groups of twenty-five stones of similar shape, thickness, and size and, using gold or silver acrylic paint, inscribed one of each of the glyphs on each stone that are outlined in Ralph Blum's *Book of Runes*. A coat or two of an acrylic spray to protect against wear and they were ready to use.

The other is our celebration of our human connection to and entwinement with the four elements of earth, air, fire, and water. Gwen held regular pledge ceremonies where we would each choose an element and the name of a mythical god or goddess that embodied both something of that element as well as attributes we would most like to emulate during the course of our pledge. We made a prayer arrow from a small, arrow-sized section of a tree branch we had picked out especially for this purpose, perhaps using a favorite tree or specific type of tree for its own symbolic qualities.

Using shells, ribbon, feathers, beads – whatever moved us creatively to symbolize our intentions – we lovingly decorated this branch and then, sitting in meditation with our completed arrow, imbued it energetically with these same intentions. Later, we would privately plant our arrow somewhere in nature to be consumed by the elements.

The day of the pledge, we donned capes and some elaborate headdresses Gwen had made and took turns saying the words of a short pledge statement she provided, pledging to experience that element in our lives for the next three years, three months, three weeks, and three days. We had completion ceremonies too, where each shared what we had learned during our previous pledge before moving on to the next of our choosing. I am now in the middle of my eighth pledge, two complete cycles of these pledges. My insights and appreciation of how elements have presented their messages to me over the years has only grown, and I plan to continue them to the end, as she did.

Through the 1990s, along with attending Gwen's Heartseek Gatherings, I also studied shamanism, Wicca, sacred geometry, astrology, and dream analysis to name a few, and the wondrous thing was how they all supported each other so beautifully. Every piece was woven into the next, making a tapestry of Oneness that I came to count on. Within this tapestry lies my truth.

Later, through Gwen's guidance, I acknowledged my intuitive abilities and, for a few years, offered intuitive readings called "Soul Stories" as an offering through our spiritually oriented group, Gateways. I gave people an intuitive reading in which a snippet of a past life came forward, something their soul wanted them to be aware of at that point in time, some piece that needed to be either incorporated into their life, or released, an opportunity for them to expand or grow in some way. I think the thing I liked best about doing that work was seeing the light go on in someone's face when they heard something that really clicked for them and they wanted to know more. I resonate with that experience; things are still "clicking" for me, and I always want to know more.

One heartwarming, yet disconcerting, thing happened many years into my relationship with Gwen. I was in San Diego to spend a week with Gwen and a group of ladies she had named "Seeking Radiance." We had been meeting there for several years, and on this particular occasion, we arrived to find Gwen had been admitted to the hospital the night before. While it seemed to be a pretty serious situation, she eventually stabilized during the course of our stay.

While we had all stayed and did what we could to enjoy our trip, Gwen was still in the hospital near the end of the week. Just before we were to all go home, she asked to see us all, a couple of people at a time. When she asked for me along with one of the other women, we walked into her darkened room expectantly. With only a short lead-in statement, Gwen clearly and unmistakably identified me as her daughter. I found I could barely breathe. It took me so by surprise that I didn't know what to think, or say, or feel, or anything. She was quite lucid, and there was no mistaking her words. The closest I can come to expressing my feelings was that, one, it was such an honor to have her say this, and two, I felt so "unworthy" to be identified in such a personal way by this woman who meant the world to me. I was on some level unable to hear it, but my friend, who had been witness to the conversation, confirmed for me that Gwen had indeed called me "daughter."

I struggled with this for some time but eventually found the courage to bring it up with her. I said I wasn't sure what she meant by it. She remembered and stood firm with her statement and then simply asked, "What does it mean to you?" Such a *very* Gwen response. "Oohhh," I moaned inside, "how can I possibly begin to answer that big question?" We did go on to discuss it further a few times. We discussed my struggle to feel worthy – not merely around my feelings for her as "Mom" but of this highly spiritual woman calling me "daughter." Eventually we found some sort of mutual territory about this new relationship of ours and established that we would be Gwen and Gloria when we were in more formal discussions, and we would be Mom and Annee (a form of my middle name) when we were speaking more casually or on a more personal level. The latter became far more dominant once we named it, and the two more or less merged as time went on.

"We spent a lot of time on footings.
We tested often for the quicksand . . .
We learned to use some unfamiliar digging tools.
So many obstacles and all so small
   compared to pleasure in her company."

— Gwenana from "Foundations of a Friendship"
   in *Inverted Trees*

Gwen's husband, John, passed away several months after Ken, and Gwen called me a few days after he died. She started by saying she was calling because I always grounded her and she was feeling so ungrounded since John passed. Then she started to cry, and through the all-too-familiar-to-me gasps for breath, she said "sometimes I . . . just . . . ca . . . can't stop." I'd never heard this woman cry before, never experienced her in need of anything emotionally.

My own breath caught for a second. I had no idea what to say to comfort her. The usual things one says would surely not do. I hurt for her and my own tears were welling up, joining hers. I took a long, deep breath and heard myself say in a mere whisper, "Oh, Gwen . . . Mom. . . I wish I were there to hold you. *Breathe honey, just breathe.*"

Her own words, spoken so many times to others who were in pain, were reflected back to her now. Then I heard two or three gulps of air on the other end of the line and a barely audible "Th-Thank you."

Almost immediately, she was Gwen again – though subdued – and we continued to talk quietly for a few minutes. It was in that moment that I knew the definition of who we were to each other had just solidified. I was no longer the student, but a peer, a friend, finally a daughter. This new relationship grew stronger from then until her death in 2013, and from that point on she always referred to me as Annee and when leaving voice mail messages I would hear, "Oh, hi Annee, this is Mom." I've saved a few just to be able to hear her voice again.

In the year after John died, we began talking quite regularly on the phone. We decided that we would each draw a Runes daily, and when we talked, compared notes on what we'd drawn, what it seemed to be telling us. We noted with particular glee when we happened to draw the same one on the same day. Later, when I went to San Diego to visit her, we did some rather elaborate tables and studied each of our full-year list of Runes, both as separate lists and how they resonated with each other. We shared a lot of oohhs and ahhhs and laughter along the way, connecting us more deeply. This speaks to me now as the way we connect through the ethers. Gwen guides my hand and speaks to me using the Runes – not choosing for me, but opening the path for me to find *the* one I need – as well as being able to answer the questions I specifically address to her, through the shared familiarity of our year with the Runes. My association of Gwen and the Runes is so strong, not only because she introduced me to them and made the set I use, but because of that year we spent exploring together, entwining our energies in this insightful and gentle oracle, paving a way for our future conversations.

Baptism, March 2010:
Of Salvation and Safety

When I asked Gwen to help me with a ceremony of baptism, she lovingly accepted, the dates were arranged, and I made my travel plans. Once I arrived at my motel in Encinitas, I connected with Gwen about a place and time, and then I set about going inward for a couple of days, looking for that voice who would lead me to what I needed. Near my motel (which was a favorite of the group when we visited Gwen) was not only a beach but a small overlook at oceanside. Nestled there, overlooking a calm blue ocean, I began to write, as had become my habit, and eventually I came up with a few baptismal statements that would serve as the beginning of the ceremony. The morning of the baptism, I found myself on the beach, walking in the warm sand and wading knee deep in the tumbling surf. It splashed all about my ankles and legs, seeming to laugh with me, celebrating this special day. I spontaneously gathered some ocean water in a small bottle I found and made my way to the park in Del Mar where I was to meet Gwen.

She soon arrived, and we settled on a nearby bench, under a shady tree, with an ocean view. She asked about my intentions for the afternoon and my journey over the last month or so as I had prepared myself for this. Nature was present as my witness: the entire time a seagull stood perched on a post nearby. Two huge ravens landed just behind us under the shade of the tree and paced back and forth. I felt they were anxious for us to begin and were keeping vigil over us. Two ground squirrels chased each other and then wandered a bit closer to us, begging for morsels of food they presumed we had for them. I gave in to their charming pleas and fed them a couple of broken up tortilla chips that had been tucked into my bag from lunch. Gwen and I laughed at their brazenness as they took the pieces gently from my fingers.

This seemed to set the stage, and I began to read the statements I'd written earlier in the day. Gwen asked a few questions along the way as a means to clarify my intent. The last statement, which turned out to be integral to the ceremony, was, "By this Sacrament I confirm that I will accept Life as it comes and welcome the Grace of Spirit, in all its forms, as a sign of my salvation." Gwen gave me a thoughtful smile and questioned the word salvation. She shared that, for her, salvation meant peace. "What does salvation mean to you?" she queried.

"I'm not sure, I replied. It was just the word that wanted to fall on the page as I wrote, and I just let it be there without questioning it."

She paused, connecting to her spiritual guides in a now familiar gesture with her hand. "I believe that for you salvation means safety."

She paused, letting the statement fall gently into my consciousness. Something deep in my core sighed, and I felt a release of an unrealized tension. Yes. Safety. I had not felt spiritually safe since Ken died. That unthinkable event had left me suspicious of life and no longer connected to "safety" as I had been before. This Baptism was to be my acceptance that no matter what, I was to trust in my Safety, through the Grace of Spirit. A door had opened that allowed me to honor all of life again, to honor my own, and Ken's, and to know that it was safe again to be alive.

"The wise man in the storm prays God, not for safety from danger, but for deliverance from fear."

—Ralph Waldo Emerson

I looked at Gwen with tears welling in my eyes, and she understood what I had seen. Smiling softly, Mother to Daughter, she saw my recognition of my Baptismal Truth, knew that I had arrived there and was ready. Taking a handful of the ocean water I had gathered earlier that morning, she released it on my head and called on Spirit to watch over me, to always show me truth, to always be my True Tribe.

After all that writing and thinking and talking, it came down to this simple moment. In response to her benediction, I concluded the ceremony with these words: "By this Sacrament I confirm that I will accept Life as it comes and welcome the Grace of Spirit, in all its forms, as a sign of my Safety." I had just taken the first formal steps toward a tentative foothold on spiritual belief, perhaps not yet walking with Spirit, but at least acknowledging Its Presence.

6

The Conjunctio

If only I am good enough,
try hard enough,
am nice enough,
understanding,
patient . . .

Then,
then I will be loved,
and understood, of course.

Try harder little girl, I tell myself,
the points you're racking up
will certainly pay off.
someday.

But maybe I'll be robbed.
The gods with whom I made this deal
may not exist.
My coins may all turn up as counterfeit.

Yet,
would this world betray someone
so good,
so nice,
who tries so hard to please?

As April and May of 2010 brought the soft warmth of spring, it also held the exploration of the second and third chakras. These sacraments of Communion and Confirmation respectively came and went without much fanfare. Myss had laid out the particulars regarding the powers contained there with typical clarity, and I seemed to breeze through both.

Second Chakra, Communion, dealt with the principal of "Honor One Another" and the idea of all of us being part of one family. It reiterated a truth I have lived by for years: that each person with whom we share a union, be that family, friends, or others, is a part of our life by Divine design. It's about learning to live with integrity within those relationships.

Third Chakra, Confirmation, is concerned with the intention to "Honor Oneself." This covers developing self-esteem, self-respect, and a survival intuition, that "listen to your gut" instinct that warns us of dangers of all kinds in our world. It speaks to an "acceptance of responsibility for the quality of person we become," says Myss.

Though I felt at the time that I understood how each of these had played out in my life, it wasn't until I hit the Fourth Chakra, and to some degree, not until I was writing this section of the book you are now reading, that the "aha" appeared and I really got it on a different level.

The Fourth Sacrament, Marriage

Having moved through the first three, or lower, Chakras, I warily began my tryst with the Fourth Chakra, the Heart Chakra. This chakra sits at the middle of the seven, linking the lower three with the upper three, linking those that ground us to the earth with those reaching for the ethereal plains. It is the chakra associated with the Sacrament of Marriage, and I could feel my reluctance to open that particular can of worms. But, having started this path, I found that I was, if nothing else, tenacious, and that I must follow this through to the end.

What I found was not what I thought was coming. I had expected a dive into marriage in a more traditional sense. I expected that all the history with my first husband and eventually finding Ken would be on my plate. I expected that I would have to look at what each had meant to me and how very different they were – both the men and the marriages. I expected a lot of things, but I didn't expect what I got.

Following is a short list of some of what Myss puts forward as the crux of the meaning of the Fourth Chakra and the Sacrament of Marriage.

> ♥ "This chakra resonates to our emotional perceptions, which determine the quality of our lives far more than our mental perceptions."

- ♥ "More than any other chakra, the Fourth represents our capacity to 'Let go and let God.' With it, "we accept our emotional challenges as extensions of a Divine plan."

- ♥ Fourth Chakra Sacred Truth: "Love is Divine Power" . . . "Each of life's challenges is a lesson in some aspect of love." "Life crises that have issues of love at their core . . . often requires, and may demand, the healing of emotional issues." "If unhealed, wounds keep us living in the past."

- ♥ "The strongest poison to the human spirit is in inability to forgive oneself . . . learning to love and forgive ourselves is a challenge to all of us . . . and therefore, our first marriage must be a symbolic one – a commitment to attend consciously to our own emotional needs . . . to live fully in self-compassion and self-forgiveness – and indeed, self-love."

- ♥ "The sacrament of Marriage is congruent with the energy of the fourth chakra. As an archetype, marriage represents first and foremost a bond with oneself, the internal union of self and soul."

As I read through this material thoroughly, I was immediately connecting to several Runes which Gwen had introduced me to so many years ago. While the idea of "the self relating rightly to The Self" runs throughout its teachings, there is one Rune, *Laguz*, (incidentally #18 in the set) which specifically came to mind as I read Myss's words. As Blum explains, "A Rune of the self relating rightly to The Self, Laguz signifies what alchemists called the *conjunctio* or *sacred marriage*."

"So this marriage thing is really about self-forgiveness? . . . self-compassion? . . . self-love?" I asked myself incredulously?! "Oh *crap!*" I said aloud. By that very response it was clear that I was in territory I obviously did not want to explore. "But what about Ken?" I wailed. "I thought this would be about a new marriage with him, across the veil? I thought we . . ." but my voice trailed away in defeat. I suddenly found myself in a very lost place, again with nowhere to turn but back.

I realized that this was to be a much deeper dive than I had thought at the onset. A new and unanticipated journey into the Sacrament of

Marriage had begun, and it was to be a joyous, painful, exuberant, tearful, blissful, angry, and turbulent process.

Over the course of two weeks or so I explored memories of my childhood, and when I discovered I had no "heart" for it, I made up some words that my head could understand, convinced myself I had done the work, and put my ceremony in place. It would take several years of going back and forth into it and hitting various walls, leaving it unfinished time and again, until, eventually, I came to the conclusion that this was not something I would ever likely be truly "done with." This part of the journey is my own Divine loop, the part of the vesica pisces that is mine to do, ever widening and ever evolving, and that it's okay, perfect in fact. I have come to understand that this loop is what my road has always been and the challenge it will likely always be – my path toward the *conjunctio*.

Tribal Input

I grew up in a Christian family, influenced mainly by my maternal side and predominantly Presbyterian. We lived in a small town in Southwest Michigan. Learning my early ethical and moral values, as many do, from family and church, I grew up, at first glance, uneventfully. Out of love and respect, and simply because it was all I knew, I continued in that vein through my childhood and early teens. By the time I turned sixteen, however, I had an inkling – an epiphany if I am to be honest – that organized religion was not for God. O ne day while in my room, doing normal teenage activities like playing music on my record player and probably dancing a bit, a totally unbidden and unrelated thought entered my barely conscious brain. I was suddenly infused with a certainty that God knew who I was, whether I was a good person or not, and that whether I went to church or not was immaterial to God. "Bad" people go to church too. Church was not necessarily for God; it was for us, whatever our reasons or motives might be. It doesn't matter to God, because we can't hide from God; God knows what lies inside, and in the bigger picture that's all that matters.

The moment passed with little more than a "wow" of recognition from my lips, and I went on about my life without giving it another thought for years, decades. I nonetheless remained the ever-respectful daughter and continued going to church each Sunday with my parents. However, during my college years, having discovered a modicum of freedom, that practice began to slip away. After I graduated, I spent the next twenty years running in the opposite direction from anything even remotely religious or spiritual, or so I thought.

As I contemplated the Fourth Sacrament, with this look into my earlier years in mind, I finally drummed up the courage to explore this history more deeply, seeking the details that might open my view to my original Confirmation and Communion sacraments, the symbolic events that shaped these rites of passage. I had long known that my Second and Third Chakras were weak, but I had not seriously looked into the whys. In addition, it seemed clear that I could not adequately delve into Marriage until I had been more intimate with the previous two. I went in search of my archetypal child and what she might be able to show me of the experiences that had molded my young psyche.

My parents were the nicest people you would ever want to meet. They were kind and caring with each other, and I always saw them as a unit; there was never one without the other. I never heard them utter an angry word toward each other, or show anything but tenderness, affection, and a gentle teasing humor. Their relationship spanned sixty-five years, beginning when my Mom was just a girl of fourteen and Dad was only seventeen. She knew on their first date that he was The One (as I did with Ken), so they grew up together, and grew old together, and died within three years of each other. Mom went first, and the pain of being without her was unbearable for my dad.

In fact, all the marriages in my family seemed strong and were enduring, and I never felt any hint of serious discord, at least until I was an older adult, looking at things with a mature eye and in retrospect. It is no surprise then that my ingrained perception was that of happy, long-lived marriages; I believed that this was how all marriages were. This was my truth from a very young age.

Also true was a sense that, as a spiritual teacher once said of me, I was "a bit of a dangling participle" in my parents' lives. It was always about them, and later I realized that, while I never doubted their love for me for a second, it nonetheless left me with a strange sense of isolation. Not lonely, but isolated, as though I was just an arm's reach away from "that kind of love" with no way to get there. I never knew that "self-love" was the path to what I yearned for in that isolation.

My early spiritual roots were founded in religion. The whole family was church-going, so there was never any reason to question the activity.

One got up on Sunday morning, dressed in something special, for me a pretty dress reserved solely for Sunday, and went to church and Sunday school. It was as normal and expected a routine as elementary school five days a week. It was what the tribe did, and I accepted it completely. Born into it, how would I know there was any other way? Rare was it that anyone even left their church for another. A cousin of mine did so as an adult of forty, the first ever in our family, as I remember.

Just before I entered fifth grade, we moved from our very small town to a somewhat larger small town, the "home town" where my maternal grandparents and many aunts, uncles, and cousins on both sides also lived. We returned to the fold, as it were, and went to the Presbyterian church my mother grew up in. That church, to this day, remains my picture of what belonging to a church feels like, what it looks like.

At thirteen, I began catechism followed by confirmation. N ow an "adult" member of the church, I joined the Junior Choir and loved singing on Sundays. I remember walking down the main aisle with the choir and seeing the huge stained glass window ahead of me. The main image in the center was of Jesus with his arms outstretched. I was mesmerized by it, and even at that age fantasized about walking down that aisle one day in a bridal gown, towards my husband-to-be, under the outstretched arms of Jesus.

When I was sixteen, that dream fell apart, and I experienced my first heartbreak. The city wanted to buy the church in order to build on that site and have all the city buildings in one general location. It nearly broke our church in half as the different factions argued for and against the sale. In the end, the church was sold and a new one built at the edge of town. The city tore down my church and built a new, modern library on its grounds. That project also required tearing down our beautiful old public library as well, one of the old original Carnegie Libraries. My friends and I often studied there, using all of the myriad reference books to write papers. It literally smelled of learning, and I loved it like a best friend. I never went in to the new one.

In an effort to appease the firestorm of emotion generated by the intense discussions regarding our church and the losing faction (where my family stood), the church leaders agreed to the extra cost of carefully removing and relocating the big stained glass window to the new sanctuary. But it was never the same. The new church, much larger and with a high, arched ceiling, made the window look small and out of place. The sanctuary felt sterile, empty, without the Presence of the old church. I did indeed get married there, but the impact was gone. It wasn't my church anymore.

"All battles in life serve to teach us something, even the battles we lose."

—Paulo Coelho, *The Fifth Mountain*

These were the first big losses in my life, and they felt like a major betrayal, leading me to the epiphany I spoke of earlier. However, I've always been quite certain that my sudden understanding that God's love was not dependent on church attendance was not manufactured as a reaction against the betrayal. The epiphany felt quite pure actually, as though God himself had whispered it in my ear. I may not have put it into these exact words at the time, but there was a revelation that God doesn't live in a building, God lives in me, and sees me warts and all, and knows my heart, whether I ever see the inside of a church again or not. While it would be some time before I truly left the church, the stage was set. I was just biding my time.

My dad's family lived farther away, in northern Indiana, and I had little direct information about his early religious background, as he never talked about that aspect of his growing up years very much. My impression was that it was somewhat evangelical in nature, though I've never been aware of any s pecifics. My paternal grandparents were good, hardworking, country people with little money and a lot of kids. There were vague stories alluding to a Shaker background some generations back, but if that is true, *somebody* must have jumped ship or I wouldn't be sitting here today. There were also stories that the family had some Native American ancestry, and my cousins and I were always excited by that notion. That may have been what led me eventually to study Native American traditions after I emerged at forty-ish from my long-held denial of Spirit.

One story that is not just a story, however, concerns my paternal grandmother, Jesse. My father and his brother would often talk so fondly of their mother, who died when I was only two. In the days when they were young boys, Jesse practiced a certain "down-home medicine" that I always imagine was somewhat prevalent on farms and in rural areas in those days early in the twentieth century. She had her own recipes for salves and poultices, and teas from roots and herbs, to cure whatever ailed you. She was also a natural healer who was very good at her craft. She was called on by folks all over the area to come and do her work, often when all else had failed.

The local doctor would sometimes drive by in his buggy and call out, "Hello Jesse! How's the family doing?" After a short, friendly conversation he would wave and tell her to call if she needed him . . . but he knew she'd probably have her own way of handling things if something *was* wrong. They appeared to be a friendly pairing, from divergent healing backgrounds, and both attended to the local community in the face of any physical adversities.

The most fascinating aspect of my grandmother's healing practice was that she did Laying on of Hands for the ill and dying. She had a piece of red yarn with a stone tied into one end of it. When called to tend to someone who was ill, she would hold it over the person's chest, letting the rock swing freely. She would ask if they believed and trusted in Jesus, and if they said "Yes," and the rock swung "correctly," she would begin to say prayers over them and lay her hands on their body where the illness seemed to lie. The prayers were mostly unintelligible to those who stood nearby. The stories I heard about Jesse claimed that the ill often did became well, and the dying became peaceful in their process. I don't know what she would do if someone said "no" to her question, but my understanding from these stories was that her powers only worked when the ill brought faith into their own healing process. Had she been born in another place and time, Jesse may have been dubbed a witch and I've always loved these stories about her. I even have a piece of her red yarn still tied to the stone she used, which carries etchings of some kind on both sides. My Dad had held onto it all those years, and it is now my treasured inheritance.

According to my dad and uncle, Jesse often told her children that this was a gift that she was to pass on through her daughters. Unfortunately, none of them, five in all, were interested. My uncle had expressed that he wanted to learn, but she either could not or would not pass it to a son.

Looking at all this now, I wonder at the road I might have taken, if she had lived longer. With my propensity for the mystical and magical, might this gift have figured in my future had I known her? If my early love of Jesus had been tapped into by Grandma Jesse, might my life have been dramatically different? Or is this, rather, a way for me to see and acknowledge that everything happens for a reason and that Jesse and I were destined to be merely kindred spirits and that my life developed as it needed to *because* these things happened exactly as they did? Whatever the truth of the matter, I know Grandma Jesse is in my DNA, and I feel a closeness to her though I have no memories of her at all.

School was another tribal experience. From the start, I enjoyed the newness of each school year, the smell of that new box of crayons, the two new dresses I shopped for with my mom, new and freshly sharpened pencils, and especially the new books and the anticipation of what I would find within those crisp new pages. I read voraciously. For years to come, my reading skills would test at two or three years past my grade level as I absorbed anything I could get my eyes on. For grades K through 2, I went to a one-room school house where copies of the textbooks for all grades (K through 8) were housed on shelves at the back of the room and available to anyone who wanted to read them. I was always in those books, following along as the grades ahead of me did their lessons with the teacher at the front of the room. I was happy soaking it all in.

I was a pretty good student, always striving for good grades and the praise I received from parents and other family. I wanted to please them, because I would feel a bit of that inclusion I so longed for at those times. This was the initial fodder for my belief that acceptance by others is a validation of my "self." I saw this pattern emerge again and again as I became a consummate people pleaser through my twenties, eager to gain acceptance into the world of whatever tribe I was trying to fit into. Whether school, family, college life, work life, or various interest groups, acceptance was key to my sense of self-worth. I learned well how to move within each to attain it.

OTTER AND DRAGON

"The difference between school and life? In school you're taught a lesson and then given a test. In life, you're given a test that teaches you a lesson."

—Tom Bodett

I always had the feeling that I was expected to go to college, a foregone conclusion, and being the people pleaser I was, off I went. In fact, I did want out of that small town, to be away from family and all that life there looked like to me. I could not have put my feelings into words then, but I knew my life had to be lived elsewhere, that I had to get away before the tentacles of tribal programming trapped me there.

The Presbyterian college I chose required freshmen and sophomores to attend church a certain number of Sundays per semester, so my departure from religion was delayed again. It was a good thing really; the church on campus was a warm, old white frame church with a tall steeple that reminded me of the comfort of my childhood church. But it was a revolving door congregation of constantly changing students and faculty that did not lend enough richness to bring me back into the fold. It was mostly an obligatory endeavor, though familiar and therefore comfortable. After college, my only visits to church occurred when I visited Mom and Dad. For their sake and for my Grandma Nora (Mom's mom) I went to church then, especially on Christmas and Easter, and I was content enough to do so because of my love and respect for them and because I did not want to rock the boat of acceptance.

College itself was a grand foray into freedom to come and go as I pleased, to study when and if I wanted to, to eat what, when, and with whom I wanted. I have happy memories of staying up late, discovering wondrous local dives like The Well (best ever cheeseburgers), getting an upperclassman to buy us beer or wine, finding a dark rural road to drink it without getting caught, going to my first frat party and smoking weed with one of my professors, laughing and shrieking in the dorm while helping to throw my roommate in the showers when she came back one night "pinned" to her boyfriend. It was almost as though the "higher learning" piece was forgotten a lot of the time, but I survived it all with a new found feeling of adulthood and anticipation, as well as a high grade point average. College was a four-year coming of age ceremony, and I relished every minute of it. As a senior I often experienced a dull ache at the thought that I would not be coming back the following autumn.

Part of that coming of age was dating, of course. A late-bloomer, I had rarely dated in high school, so I was rather unseasoned in the art of figuring out the opposite sex as I launched into this phase. I quickly learned some hard lessons about boys and dating that most of my girlfriends had learned in high school. All in all, looking back, I see us all as so very young. Neither girls nor boys knew squat about anything, but we thought we knew it all – as is probably true for the youth of any generation. With this in mind, I now look back fondly at the man-boys who were part of my college days. One, however, did stand out, and he was the biggest challenge of any of them.

Andy and I met while I was dating John in my freshman year. John brought me to The Union one evening to meet some friends with whom he played Hearts after dinner most nights. The group was so large that sometimes we had to play triple-deck Hearts in order to accommodate the crowd. It was a really great time. After unexpectedly finding John with someone else one evening, it was over with us, but I was determined not to lose these new friends I'd found because of him. I steeled myself every night and showed up on my own. Perhaps it made John uncomfortable or perhaps it was clear how much the group welcomed me even after the breakup, but it didn't take long before he and his new girlfriend eventually quit the group.

This became a turning point. I'd found my place; I, uncharacteristically, stood my ground because I knew this was where I belonged, with this gregarious and eclectic bunch of people, my tribe for the duration of my college years and for some time beyond.

Over time, the larger crowd dwindled, and Hearts turned into Bridge. There was always at least one table going, and we kibitzed and changed partners throughout the day as people came and went, to and from class. The group spanned all of my college years, and none of us ever went Greek, so eventually we consecrated ourselves a "frarority" called the GDI's (God Damned Independents), and proud to be so.

The Quest for Relationship Begins

Andy was one of the GDIs, and we became a casual, off-and-on couple for two years, working through immaturity and jealousies and feelings of betrayal along the way. I was eventually ready for something "real," but it seemed he was not, and his occasional wandering, which he tried to hide, always came to light. A couple of times I went out with someone else just for spite, to see if it mattered to him. It did. Either way, we would argue, then not talk at all, yet somehow, we always came back to each other and went on. During our senior year something shifted. He seemed to settle in and settle down, and the casualness of our relationship slipped into a guarded commitment. We visited each other during breaks and met each other's parents and began to talk about the future.

After graduation, I moved to the Detroit area, following Andy who began graduate school at Wayne State. I thought about grad school briefly as well, even getting accepted for an American Lit program at Wayne, but I decided to postpone it while Andy finished his degree. There was plenty of time for that. And if we were to be able to marry anytime soon, I needed a job in order to contribute enough so we could afford our own place.

I spent a year working as a bank teller, but I left that enthusiastically when a friend from college called one day to tell me that her department at Parke, Davis & Company needed someone who knew a little Spanish; she thought I was a good fit. With one year of Spanish in college, I interviewed and got the job. I would spend the next thirty years there through its various iterations as Warner-Lambert and Pfizer. It was a major "corporate America experience" for which I am grateful. Despite its unique political nature, and the shortcomings of such an arena, it gave me a good living and allowed me to focus on my often confusing, sometimes enriching, and always challenging, outside life. In short, it was another tribe I learned how to navigate.

Meanwhile, Andy and I continued to expand our relationship. I met his two best friends, and their girlfriends, and they all became my friends as well and an integral part of my life for many years.

I was twenty-five when Andy and I married, and I felt secure going into it. We had known each other for a long time now and had already, it appeared, worked through a lot of issues. Why would I ever doubt our rightness for each other? Besides, marriage was what couples *do*.

And, don't forget, my view of marriage was idyllic given my childhood perceptions of the institution. I thought the happily-ever-after phase of life had begun. That illusion was short lived.

We were married in July 1972. By Christmas I was worried.

After our wedding, Andy almost immediately distanced himself from me physically. Though I had nothing to compare it to, I had always thought we had a good sex life, and now it was in trouble for no reason I could comprehend. My skills at talking about this issue were nil, and we rarely discussed it. I experienced an uncomfortable unfamiliarity in dealing with what I had heard termed as 'the fragile male ego'. The bottom line was that this beget a silence that was to become the beginning of the end for us and assured a distancing of two people who had once seemed so right for each other. We became good roommates, each taking up whatever household duties we had talent for and going about our social engagements with no one the wiser about our private life. I eventually sought professional help to try to save us, but he refused to join me, saying, "All they want to do is mess with your head." Then I kept busy with friends from work and other pursuits that kept me away from home when I knew he'd be there. He seemed to do the same. We stayed married for ten years, bent on continuing because marriages must endure, but we also continued to hurt each other with our silence, and our ineptness, and our fear of any real communication.

He had two affairs. I didn't learn about them until late in the marriage, but it was a slap in the face, given the distance between us in the bedroom. I tried on several occasions to talk to him, but to no avail. With little to no involvement on his part in trying to solve our marital problems, it became clear to me that I couldn't possibly be more miserable single than I had become in this marriage. There seemed no way through this mess we had created. I had a brief flirtation with someone I met through my work but hated living that way. That and the therapist helped me clarify things however, and I eventually moved out, divorcing him shortly after our tenth anniversary.

Finally free to be free, and in an attempt to determine if the fault had been mine and to re-establish some modicum of feminine self-esteem again, I launched into dating with a vengeance. Over the next fifteen years, I managed to navigate, and sometimes none too well, three other reasonably long-term relationships. I didn't understand what kept going wrong and always read it as *my* failure.

It was through this process that I noticed I had been living my life backwards, or at least inside-out. While dating virtually not at all in high school, I had dated a little in college, though very short term and nothing had been serious besides Andy. I had gone to college, married the first man I ever really knew, and *then* my learning curve about myself, and men, and relationships began. What I knew of relationships was all out of whack, tangled in a ball of roots that had formed my tree of knowledge as a *child*, and that had not grown much since. I felt confused and lost. I couldn't see the truth of what had always gone so wrong for me in relationships and desperately wanted to put all this into perspective, like a grown up woman, before the tree totally uprooted.

My first step, after the string of relationships ended, was to look at them as clearly as I could to seek whatever I may have learned from each experience. I so needed to find out who I was, because at the very least it was clear that I had been living my life for and through the men I had dated. I knew precious little about *me*. I'd spent so much time trying to prove myself to them, to please them, to be fully accepted by them, that I had lost all sense of who I was, just me, Gloria. I took on their interests, their hobbies, their likes and preferences, and I lost any real sense of my own. I'd been their perfect match; so why had I failed at every relationship I'd ever been in?

I blamed myself for somehow missing the clues, being wrong about what had been needed, for not being what *they* needed me to be. I felt unable to provide what a good relationship required, as though it all fell on my shoulders, inherently mine to do, like a job description. I finally began to see, however, that my people-pleasing tendencies and lack of a strong sense of self-esteem were at the hub of these "failed" relationships. This was something I figured out long before I delved into the Sacraments, but I revisited these revelations as part of my 2010 endeavor.

Throughout my forties and fifties, I continued to yearn for *the* relationship, one that more fully reflected what I had seen between my parents. I always felt an emptiness in that part of my life, always the shadow of something that it seemed could never be mine. I didn't understand why, but while the rest of my life was moving along smoothly, this one aspect, this one little ache, was always present. I wanted the kind of closeness my parents had; I wanted many, many good and happy years with someone, someone who "knew me when," someone to share everything with, to share my deepest self with, to trust with the entirety of me.

This was the woman I had become inside. I was not lonely per se; I had many friends and a full and generally happy life. But I still endured this sense of isolation, of a hole that nothing ever really seemed to fill. I simply expected that it would remain so, and, at some point, envisioned a life of singlehood until I died.

Spirit Speaks

Throughout my years of relationship experimentation, I slowly, without intention, began to develop a peripheral interest in things occult: gypsy fortune telling, astrology, witchcraft, magic – things that seemed mysterious and outside the realm of my "normal" world. I told myself that it was just an interesting side bar to my life, a hobby of sorts, but eventually I had to acknowledge it was more.

It was in the mid-eighties that I began attending classes through Michigan Metaphysical Society, and I became hooked. I met so many interesting people and wanted to know more about everything. It was like someone had lit a fire in me and I only wanted to add more kindling. However, this spiritual experimentation still remained a separate piece of my life. There was "making a living," "having a social life," and this . . . this other thing I was investigating. Years would pass before the light bulb went on: that this was to be *integrated* into my life, not kept in a separate little box labeled "other."

Somewhere in the late eighties, while roaming a metaphysical bookstore, I saw a flyer about a Sioux teacher who was coming to town. I began working with him through a spiritual group that sponsored him in Michigan. This resonated like nothing ever had. I felt as if I'd done this before, been here before; I felt at home. A sense of peace came over me when I listened to the flute music, and my feet naturally moved to the drums at the pow-wows. That Native American background has been my spiritual bedrock ever since, the place I go when I need grounding.

A year or so later, I was introduced to the spiritual healer and teacher Dennis Adams, and I attended several of his events. I also began to routinely utilize animal/nature symbolism, doing many workshops with Ted Andrews. Dreams, numerology, and the study of tarot became a mainstay in order to investigate life circumstances. I became a sort of poster child for the spiritually eclectic. Without really being aware of it, or having any intention of undertaking a spiritual journey, I was on my way; I was looking for my path to Spirit, to God, to The All That Is. Not long after this, I was introduced to Gwen's Heartseek Gatherings.

"A disciple can never imitate the steps of his guide, because each of us has our own way of seeing life, of coping with difficulties and with victories. Teaching is merely showing that something is possible. Learning is making something possible for yourself."

—Paulo Coelho, *The Diary of a Magus*

When I met Gwen in 1993, I knew she would change my life by opening me to the enormity of Spirit. Gwen gave me permission to explore my own understanding of the spiritual world and how it operates on earth. She never claimed to have *the* truth, but she shared *her* truth, and counseled us again and again to run it through our own "circuits," take what rang true, and leave the rest. She had no investment in how or what we chose but worked with each of us where we were. Since truth always resonates with truth, and mine regularly resonated with hers, Gwen's teachings served as a kind of litmus test for other teachers or teachings. If it sounded like a record player needle slashing through the grooves of a record, instead of Mozart, I knew it wasn't for me.

The Song of The Dragon

Using that metaphor, I guess I'd say that dragons are like Mozart to me. In 1996, I went to see the movie *DragonHeart*. For some reason I was drawn to go alone. As I entered the theater and sat down, I felt an uneasy tension that continued into the first scene. Before the dragon, Draco, was even introduced, I felt certain he was going to die and, inexplicably, tears welled up at the thought of it. To the plus side, Sean Connery was the voice of the dragon, and that voice captivated me. I deemed it how any self-respecting male dragon should sound. That voice made Draco real.

The plot was established, the usual good versus evil with a little humor thrown in. The knight and dragon work through their issues, eventually become friends, and band together to fell the evil prince. As I knew it would, the movie ends with the death of the dragon doing the brave and honorable thing. His spirit rises into the night sky and becomes the eye in the constellation Draco.

Through the last scenes, my chest was tight with pain. When it was over, I hurried out the back door of the theater. *If anyone sees me crying, they'll think I'm nuts*, I thought. *Stop it, it was just a movie! I never cry at movies!* But this was such an anomaly that I couldn't ignore the reaction. I sat in my car, crying my eyes out because he was the *last* dragon, and he was dead, and they were gone forever! Of course I knew this was the fictional script of a movie, but my emotions were having none of the reality of that realization. As inexplicable as this all sounds, ever since, I have felt an affinity for dragons. I can't help but feel that in some time now long past, dragons were indeed real, they had existed, and I knew them. Then they were gone, relegated to myth and legend and while they were usually touted as the bad guys; I knew better.

I began to read about dragons, exploring my sudden sense of connection. I learned that most people know dragons as mythical creatures and, depending on the culture involved, they were either dangerous monsters to be slain (European legends) or protective beings of great wisdom (China and the Far East). Worldwide, dragons are symbolic as a source of energy, healing, oracular powers, and immortality. True believers in the Faerie tradition usually include dragons in this realm as well.

A few years later, D.J. Conway's *Dancing with Dragons* gave me further insights. Conway writes, "It has been my experience that, although dragons have form and existence, they do not exist in this physical world as we do. Dragons inhabit the astral plane that co-exists with and inter-penetrates this physical plane. Astral beings are as real as we are; they just have a body that vibrates at a different rate than physical matter here does." Had this movie reminded me of something on a soul level? Had I somehow accessed ancient memory, lived with them in some parallel universe? How else could I explain such strong feelings that were so unlike me? I don't know, and perhaps I never will, but discovering dragons has changed my perception of anything that

79

is now routinely defined as myth, legend, imagination, or storytelling of any kind. I have come to simply accept my belief in these wondrous beings and cherish my unusual relationship with them, including them as a very personal totem.

I have learned to embrace the eccentricity of this quirk in my personality, and yes, I do believe they are real, though mostly invisible to us in this dimension; and that once upon a time, in some other world or past life, we were very special friends. I am pleased that we remain so. These days I have a happy collection of them all over my house: pictures, books, figurines, note cards, and garden statuary. Two stuffed animals, an otter and a dragon, sit on top of the TV armoire in my bedroom. I have two copies of *DragonHeart*, which I've nearly worn out, and *How To Train Your Dragon* is now also on my list of favorite movies. And, of course, there's the dragon tattoo on my right shoulder.

Ken's Life Before Me

When I was born, Ken was already three years old, growing up in a small town in Illinois. While he had three siblings and I had none, our early years held some of the same kind of experiences. Family, school, church all figured prominently in his life too. H e w as a good student, likely exceptional with his IQ, and way out of my league intellectually. His left brained scientist and my right brained artistic soul nonetheless found synchronicity.

After Ken passed, I found some notes he'd written that indicated he had considered becoming a minister in his younger years and the spiritual bond we shared began to make more sense. This was something he'd never told me about. For various reasons, he instead found a far different calling in the sciences and eventually earned his Ph.D. there. During several moves within the pharmaceutical industry, he worked his way up from the laboratory bench to an executive's desk. Over the years, he made many friends at work and became a positive influence for those seeking a career in that industry. Ken was gregarious and had a healthy curiosity about things, especially about people, and he used that to advantage during his tenure in the industry. Not one to exhibit the usual "corporate leadership style," Ken was often told his unusual management style "shouldn't work," but to the amazement of his bosses, he and his teams flourished, using his own brand of communication, ethics, and attentive approach.

Ken's early roots within the church continued to be an important part of his life, and he attended a local Methodist church regularly. This provided him the spiritual solace his heart and soul needed. Somewhere along the way, as his personal life underwent stresses, he found himself in a dual path of exploration into Gestalt therapy and Buddhism. With Gestalt, his sharpness and intelligence made it easy for him to grasp the concepts and apply them to his life, both business and personal. His study and practice of Buddhism afforded him a sort of philosophy, as he explained it to me, which eased some of the pressures he was under. He found that the three practices were mutually supportive, giving him a firm foundation on which to rebuild himself and his life.

I must say here that Ken's past is not mine to tell, nor his secrets mine to share. He had his demons, as we all do, and he shared deeply with me about them in the short time we had together. We both understood, especially at our age, that relationships come with baggage on both sides, and we both carried our share. In order to honor our trust in each other, I will offer no more of his background here. My intention is not to make him a saint but only to share my story and my experience – and, in truth, I did get the very best of him.

I can share that Ken was so proud of his kids, and he was proud of his ability to provide for them and, at the time I met him, to be able to give them a home, be supportive of them as young adults, and be a dad. All of his family was of paramount importance to Ken: his kids and their spouses, his grandchildren, his siblings and their spouses and kids, and now me. He even adopted my ninety-year-old aunt as his own; you could tell he enjoyed her very much and was charmingly attentive to her and her needs.

Wedding Bells

One day in mid-June 2009, Ken was resting on the couch, and I was sitting in a nearby chair. We were talking about things in general. Gwen would be in town soon, and I was preparing to host the Gathering; Ken was tying up loose ends at work. I don't remember what triggered it – probably some reference to his illness or his chemo treatments – but suddenly, with a rush of emotion welling up in me, I bolted out of my chair, leapt to his side, and blurted out, "I want to be your wife!" He looked at me kneeling there at his side, our eyes locked in a now familiar bond; with his eyes soft and teary, he smiled, and without hesitation quietly murmured, "I want that too."

In a split second we had gone from the "Merger", to maybe we'd get around to it at some point, to *now, we need to do this now.*

I got the license the next day. There was no discussion about the how or where or content of the ceremony or who to invite. We didn't even have a date. We just felt the sudden urgency to do it. And I felt an inexplicable desire to take his name.

A few days later, Ken needed to go to the emergency room to deal with a chemo-related issue. While we were waiting, he took out a tablet of paper and began writing intently. I didn't ask him about it then, but he read it to me a few days later. As he read, I realized it was a marriage proposal.

Although I had blurted out my desire to be his wife, Ken's words confirmed it was his wish as well. He told me that he had to come to terms with something before he could be fully in sync with our marriage, and it had nothing to do with me or his love for me. This is what he wrote.

The Proposal:

Right Arm/Left ArmThursday, June 18, 2009

> "I have this recurring need to apologize that I am sick. All I want to do is make Gloria happy and being seriously ill does not do that (if my serious illness is how I define myself). Besides bringing some sadness to her, it also adds some burden due to the time and energy related to dealing with my illness and related care. I realize being sorry or needing to apologize doesn't make any sense. So I have been struggling with my need to apologize and the silliness of that belief and to understand the learning that is being offered.
>
> Sitting here now, I realize that it would make no sense for my right arm to apologize to my left arm for taking it to the ER. Both of my arms are me and I cannot go anywhere without both of them. We are all in this together. This must mean that my need to apologize to Gloria reflects some lack of understanding/

appreciating the fact that we are one! That is a degree of love and connection that I have never understood before, let alone experienced.

My only reservation about marrying Gloria was my concern that without some understanding about what I have done "wrong" in the past, I may be doomed to repeat past behavior and ruin the best thing that has ever happened to me.

While I don't have all the answers to what I have done "wrong," I believe I have a clear sense of a big fork in the road and of taking a totally different path now.

Having this sense of a new vision and understanding of what it really means for a right arm and left arm to be different but still part of a single organism, I can understand the road with Gloria, where we are really an integrated person. We are one!

I realize our life is a journey and we have gotten this far by traveling the road with trust and honesty and that we will grow what we have to a new height of joy and happiness. With this understanding I am ready to move on. Will You Marry Me?"

Surrender:

Friday, June 19, 2009, approximately 10 am in the Sun Room

"Being in love is a total surrender – much like a Christian must surrender to God.

Total surrender at first seems to mean being totally vulnerable and is, if the one to whom you are surrendering doesn't have the best interest of the two individuals that make the one, and the one they create in their heart. While the surrender seems risky from the outside – it is the ONLY way to experience that feeling that comes from being "in love" and experience the joy that can come from being one. Will You Marry Me?"

Gwen arrived the following Friday. I was readying the house for the Gathering and feeling nervous and unsettled. Ken and I had told very few people what was going on with his health, but Gwen and a few close friends knew. Many other friends would also be there, and I felt I needed to tell everyone about it, since I'd known them all for years, and I did not want to dance around it and be vague all weekend. Once we had come together in Circle, I took a deep breath and managed to convey the news without crying, including our intended marriage. Once it was done, the synchronicity of events came as quickly and easily as if the whole thing had been laid out well in advance.

*"I promise to love you as my self and to retain
my individuality. I promise to be honest with you
at all times, even when doing so seems scary,
because we are on a new road, and 'scary' is just
another word for 'we have not been here before.'"*

Gloria and Ken, June 29, 2009,
with Reverend Lorna Brown performing
their wedding ceremony

Spirit was certainly present and active in the timing, and we all felt the magic in every moment. First, that we had been struck by the marriage plan just the week before Gwen's arrival and then got the license right away. With the announcement about his health and marriage plans, all the love in the room began to form a veritable ball of energy that manifested a wedding almost before our very eyes. With a wink and a nod, Universe provided the final nudge. Gwen's flight plans had been "oddly" put askew. Normally, she came in on a Friday, did the workshop Saturday and Sunday, and left on Monday. *Somehow*, her return flight had inadvertently ended up on Tuesday instead, and she had a whole extra day "with nothing to do." And Monday was my Mom and Dad's anniversary date, June 29.

Within a few moments, we were planning our wedding for Monday. My wonderful friends took the lead and began putting the plans together, each taking a special piece of the day as their own. We would have it at the house, and Lorna, the ordained minister in the group, would marry us. Ken wore his tux and was my handsome groom. I matched his tux with a long black and white dress I found in my closet, fit for the bride. Gwen walked me down the aisle and gave me away, and we were married in front of the fireplace, underneath the painting of Grandmother Moon, where it seemed all our most significant dates had happened.

"We often think that when we have completed our study of one we know all about two because two is one and one. We forget that we still have to make a study of and."

—A. Eddington, *The Nature of Physics.*

I had brought to our ceremony a mesh-like, woven silver Guatemalan wedding necklace that a friend had given me many years before. It was of ample length to be wrapped around both of our necks as we faced each other. (Such was its intention within the indigenous community where it originated.) Holding hands and looking into each other's eyes, we spoke our vows within the circle of that necklace and the circle of those present. We both had tears in our eyes, tears of joy for this ceremony, for our oneness and twoness being formally united.

Ken's vows included the words of the proposal he had written earlier. Mine were, in part, as follows:

Kenneth – Our journey together as we come to its fruition in marriage reminds me of our countless conversations on oneness and twoness and the symbol of the vesica pisces. Nothing seemed more natural than to include this in my vows today.

The vesica pisces, like two wedding rings overlapped against each other, symbolizes our marriage. Two equal circles. Kenneth and Gloria, the edge of each touching the others center, it is an ancient symbol, signifying a source of strength and power. This silver necklace that encompasses us as we stand here, represents the eye of that vesica pisces and was generated by our journey together, the space we share "apart" from our individuality, yet "a part" of the whole. Just as each has touched the heart of the other, our own selves remain intact while creating a sacred shared space of togetherness. This sacred space was birthed from our past and our future, yielding a oneness that is unique unto itself while supporting the oneness of each of the two. It is a conscious and ongoing creation, like the union of heaven and earth, whose energy is neither one nor the other but a strong and powerful mingling of the two, with the power and force of Love at its center.

I was recently reminded of a chant that I learned years ago that took on a new layer of meaning when I applied it to our ceremony today. As I sing it now, I offer it to you, Kenneth My Love, as a heartfelt prayer for our union, for our trust and belief in each other, and in the process of that union.

> *"I am a circle; I am healing you.*
> *You are a circle; you are healing me.*
> *Unite us; Be One.*
> *Unite us; Be as One."*

We concluded with these words:

> *"I promise to love you as my self and to retain my individuality. I promise to be honest with you at all times, even when doing so seems scary, because we are on a new road, and 'scary' is just another word*

for 'we have not been here before.' This ring, forming a complete and unbroken circle, itself a symbol of eternity, having no beginning and no end, I now give to you as a token of our love for each other."

We were palpably present with each other, as we stood together that day and I felt one heartbeat sustaining us both. I vividly remember nearly every detail of the day and can still feel us swaying together as we danced our wedding dance to John Denver's "For You."

My Life As An Ostrich

Early in our relationship, Ken told me he was writing a book called *My Life As An Ostrich*. He was, of course, referring to the myth (yup, it's a myth) that when confronted with something scary, or dangerous, or onerous, an ostrich will bury it's head in the sand to hide from it. It was a metaphor Ken felt he had lived for some time. He wanted to share his insights and his journey to encourage others to leave that pattern behind. I never found his notes on the book, but he referenced it often enough that I had a sense of what he was going for.

I have certainly had my own share of ostrich moments in life, so my experience with denial was, well, undeniable. We had shared many conversations about each of our past bouts with knowing something was wrong, or in need of attention, needing to *do* something to right the situation, yet somehow often just filing it away to deal with "tomorrow." I called them my "Scarlett" moments.

The day Ken told me the cancer had returned ushered in another phase of denial for both of us. Despite our many promises to "not do the same thing" as in previous relationships, we both reacted like ostriches in the face of his diagnosis and the increasing severity of his illness.

We seemed to leap in unison to the same page – the one titled, "We're going to beat this, and we aren't going to even talk about the what-ifs." We never really did, until quite late in the process, perhaps too late by then. I admit with some incredulity that one week prior to his death was the first time I actually uttered the words "Ken is going to die – and soon."

For many months after he died, I berated myself for my lack of awareness and courage; I spent a lot of time during the dark days kicking myself. I agonized over the lost opportunity for rich and meaningful conversations that would have been in keeping with the kind of relationship we wanted and the kind of spiritual life journeys we both valued. I longed for answers to questions that I never dared ask until it was all over. Angry at myself, and feeling guilty at denying him the chance to express all that he must have been feeling and holding in, I apologized to him often, for what seemed like months after he passed. I was also angry at him for not forcing me early on into the conversations routinely avoided.

It was only about two years ago (eight years after Ken's death) that I re-read his proposal, the "Right Arm, Left Arm" piece, and the truth hit me like a freight train: There was no need to apologize; there was nothing to forgive, nothing to repay. I hadn't opened those conversations . . . and neither had he. And likely he'd felt as bad about it as I had. We had both participated in "ostrich-ism." We had chosen that path together, as the unit that we were. This was so simple, and so major, that I felt a rush throughout my entire body as this truth settled in on me. A tension I'd been holding lifted. I felt Ken there with me, as real as he'd been on our wedding day.

On reflection, perhaps our mutual denial allowed us to focus more on healing and enjoying the days we did have, instead of being mired in the what-ifs. I am reminded that there is always a bigger picture to consider, and trusting in the perfection of that has been key to my own healing. Gwen whispers in my ear, "You can't do it wrong. Neither of you did it wrong."

It was then that I recalled a conversation with Ken from early in our relationship. We were sitting in the Sun Room on a lovely spring day, coffee in hand, a soft, sweet breeze wafting through the open windows, caressing us. It was just before he left for work that morning, and he said something to me about appreciating that I never seemed to look back – only forward. He admired that I did not dwell on the past, but focused on the future and what was to come, that I anticipated with a positive mindset. With my latest realization, I knew Ken was standing near me. I was sure he had dropped that memory into my head at just that moment to make a point. I heard myself ask, "What has happened to me; where has that woman gone?" In that split second, I found myself on a quest to resurrect in myself the mindset that Ken loved so much, get over my self-imposed guilt trip, and live the life he would want me to have.

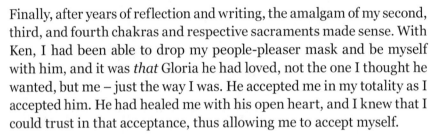

*"Even after all this time, the sun never says to the earth,
'You owe me.'
Look what happens with a love like that.
It lights the whole world."*

—Hafiz

Finally, after years of reflection and writing, the amalgam of my second, third, and fourth chakras and respective sacraments made sense. With Ken, I had been able to drop my people-pleaser mask and be myself with him, and it was *that* Gloria he had loved, not the one I thought he wanted, but me – just the way I was. He accepted me in my totality as I accepted him. He had healed me with his open heart, and I knew that I could trust in that acceptance, thus allowing me to accept myself.

I could see it now, feel it, and was now able to forgive myself for all the guilt I'd carried, for all the times I felt I failed him. Right arm, left arm: nothing to forgive. This knowing was my private ceremony, finally completing the Marriage Sacrament started way back in 2010.

This would not be the last time it took me years to complete one of those sacraments.

7

Completion

Take as a talisman
a lizard which has lost its tail.
It is completely unimpaired by battle scars
of which it has no understandings nor regrets
and so lives on
as though it still was whole.
And thus becomes.

The hot summer months of 2010 marched on and, as in a call and response manner, so the last two sacraments heated up my spiritual path. July came and went and with it the 5th Chakra and the Sacrament of Confession.

Myss states that this sacrament is about surrendering personal will to Divine Will. "This surrender is the greatest act we can perform to bring spiritual stability into our lives. Every one of us has some awareness that . . . life contains a Divine plan. The fifth chakra is the center for that awareness and for our desire to make contact with the Divine plan." "Regardless of the specific crisis, we find ourselves in a situation that *forces us to confront the limitations of our own inner resour*ces . . ." She states that aligning our will to that of the Divine "*allows Divine authority to enter our lives and reorder our struggles into successes and our wounds into strengths.*"

Ahhh, I still had a ways to go. I had come to an understanding with Ken, but God was still another matter. Could it be as simple as accepting that what had happened to Ken and me was just part of a Divine Plan? Nothing personal in it? Thinking I understood, while basically unaware that the original resentments were still clutching at me, I quickly moved through a sham of a ceremony and continued my trek. A telling commentary is that I knew it had been a sham but I didn't care and wanted to just move on. Gwen deftly stepped in and reminded me to trust the process. "Trust Timing; you can't do it wrong," she said.

As I relaxed into that statement, I was reminded of something that happened one day, late in Ken's chemo treatments. Early one morning, while Ken was still sleeping, I had gotten up and busied myself with some household chores. This was a necessary and practical matter but also kept my mind occupied. It was in part due to simple nervous energy at that point, but the busy-ness also both served my denial and kept my emotions in check, as I was determined not to burden Ken with constant breakdowns.

Many mornings, before our routine of getting him moved from bed to couch and hopefully eating some oatmeal, I would sit on the sun porch and cry. Unable to focus on my chores, I did so that morning. I felt so helpless, watching the relentless downhill slide of his energy and weight loss, unable to do anything to change the course of things for this man whom I loved beyond words.

I found myself unwilling to share my feelings with him as we always had before, so afraid I'd rob him of whatever fight he still had left. I did not want him to go back to blaming himself for my misery, wasting precious energy on something so beyond our control. I recalled the passage in his wedding vows: "Right arm; Left arm" . . . a beautiful insight but I could not be certain it would hold up through this; I needed to protect him in whatever small ways I could.

But then, something shifted slightly as I sat there. Unable to identify that shift in the moment, or perhaps because I heard Ken and needed to go to him, I forgot all about this unexpected change in my demeanor when I went back to the bedroom to say good morning.

I stood at the foot of the bed and held his feet. I've no idea why or how that started but it had become a habit. I believe it was my attempt to ground him into the world, to be sure he was firmly planted here and that he felt his own presence and connectedness. As we looked into each other's eyes, a few simple words came to me with surprising assurance. "You healed me," I said.

"You healed me too," he immediately replied with a soft smile.

It was as though we had just finished a long intimate talk and nothing more needed saying. He knew it too; I could see it in his eyes.

Coming back from this memory a question occurred to me: Could all of this have been a Divine Set-up? Was this the answer to my lingering issues around the Fifth Sacrament? Had the Plan always been about our healing each other? Healing not only our wounds from previous relationships but ultimately our God-wounds? We both had a history of God-wounds, maybe we all do, but certainly surrender was his challenge with God now, as was mine, and we walked that path together, as always. It seemed that our foray into oneness and twoness included much more than we'd been aware of at the start; we were here "for each other" in the bigger picture as well. How this healing took place is part of the Mystery but within that silent conversation, we had said it all.

"Relinquishing control is the ultimate challenge for the Spiritual Warrior. . . . Willingness and permitting are what this Rune requires . . . and calls for no less an act of courage than an empty-handed leap into the void."

— Ralph Blum, from "The Blank Rune" in *The Book of Runes*

I moved seamlessly into my memory of another conversation Ken and I had near the end. It was September, and we had just come back from a doctor's appointment where Ken had been given three to six months to live. We had been told to go home and call hospice. When we got back to the house, after a shaky and wordless drive home, we sat in our now familiar eye to eye/holding hands position. We both cried. Then he said, "So, three to six *months.*" Hoping he still had some fight left, I replied, "That's what *they* say."

His response was swift and stated with a conviction I'd not heard in his voice for a while: "Then what's the point?"

Three *weeks* later, he was gone.

As I considered this during meditation, I came to a stunning conclusion: *He was doing much more in that moment than giving up!* I found myself thinking again in a bigger picture perspective. We had healed each other as best we could up to then. His healing would continue on the other side. But mine, he knew, was only just starting, here, and his staying would not further that particular journey. His soul, so aware of my own at that point, knew that the only way for my healing to begin was for him to leave.

I've come to believe that, as we get closer to death, we are closer to God than our earthly reality, and thereby more tuned in to things beyond our awareness in normal life. Ken had made contact with the Divine Plan and let go of life in full acceptance of it. Not only for his own healing, but for mine. As Myss had stated of this sacrament, alignment with the Divine "allows Divine authority to enter our lives and reorder our struggles into successes and our wounds into strengths." These two brief conversations between us spoke clearly of our shared fifth chakra healing path. Tears streamed down my face as I remembered his reference to surrender in his wedding vows and with this realization I experienced the magnitude of what love and surrender can truly mean.

Sixth Chakra, Sacrament of Ordination

In August I began to pursue the next chakra, the Sixth. I did a cursory read of the Myss material and was not quite grasping what she was saying, or more accurately, how it pertained to my situation. Then, there it was. In a short passage, Myss writes: "It is by Divine design that we ask 'Why?' and want to know more today than we did yesterday. The energy pulsating from this chakra continually directs us to evaluate the truth and integrity of our beliefs." She continues, "The sacrament of Ordination, in the literal sense, is the act of being made a priest and officially taking up the life task of channeling the sacred."

Also, "Human reasoning can never answer the mysteries of our lives." There is a complexity to understanding why things happen as they do that only the Divine can comprehend. Only by embracing trust in that can we experience the sacred in life and the peace we so desire. "Trust, trust, trust", as Gwen would say.

A LOVE STORY

———— ✵ ————

"No one knows what is going to happen in the next few minutes, and yet people still go forward, because they have trust, because they have faith."

—Paulo Coelho, *Brida*

———— ✵ ————

The Sacrament of Ordination was the only date I orchestrated in order to coincide with an actual ordination that was to take place in North Carolina, near the Smoky Mountains, on August 8, 2010. It was also the only one where I did the ceremony first, and intended the "work" to be done once I returned home. I had known from the beginning of this process in March that I wanted a legal ordination to be my ceremony for this sacrament. Two friends of mine had been ordained some years before by a man named Dan Chesbro, whose church, Sanctuary of The Beloved, was in upstate New York. It spoke to me clearly as the path I was to take, with Dan presiding. I researched his schedule to find dates and locations where he would be conferring ordinations, and I found one in North Carolina in August, the month of my study of the sixth sacrament.

Spirit supported this decision by sending me a spiritual traveling companion. My friend, Nancy, for reasons of her own, decided to join me for the weekend-long Ordination Ceremony, and we made somewhat of a vacation out of it by extending the trip to a week and meandering our way through the Smoky Mountains as part of our preparation for the ceremony.

On the way down, as we took the road through the western edge of the mountains, I wanted to find the spot where I had taken the picture of Ken with the red streak running through it. Nancy, being very sensitive and aware of the energies of those on the Other Side, made a point of including Ken in our conversations, and as we parked at the spot, she said, "C'mon Ken, let's go. You need to see this place again too!" We walked to the short stone wall that rimmed the edge along a steep crevice overlooking the river below. We sat on the wall a few feet from where Ken had been sitting in the picture and looked around. I didn't really know specifically what we were looking for, but certainly a sign of some sort that Ken was here too, a confirmation that he had indeed joined us on this trip.

We both took what happened next as a magical, mystical experience. As I sat there, a couple of blue butterflies began flitting about us. I put my hand out and cooed, "Well hello there, beautiful." Within seconds the blue butterfly landed on my hand, walked onto my index finger and settled in. Nancy and I looked at each other wide-eyed, wordlessly expressing our mutual belief that Ken had found a way to be with us in a very real way. The butterfly was not leaving anytime soon. I moved my hand in to look more closely, and still it did not move. I held it up a bit so Nancy could take a picture – still there. A few other tourists happened to notice and came over for a picture. Ken stayed on my finger for more than five minutes, lingering and lounging there long enough to be sure we were sure, and while we still lingered at that spiritually high altitude, the blue butterfly flitted into the air, danced around a bit, and slowly drifted away. We were giddy with the experience.

I have often heard that in spiritual matters, the big things are usually small, and the small things are actually big. This apparently held true for my ordination trip. That small blue butterfly had such an impact, while the big ceremony with Dan Chesbro felt fairly ordinary. I don't mean to diminish it in any way. It was a lovely ceremony, and I felt quite "complete" having had that experience; it had a gentle impact on both of Nancy and me, and we talked more about that on the drive home. But the butterfly . . . I still get goosebumps.

It would be later in August when I realized that this "ordinary" Ordination had opened the very door for me that Myss had indicated. With the blue butterfly I had experienced, (or perhaps channeled?), a sacred encounter, and inexplicably was no longer asking "why." I continued, as I still do, to enjoy the speculations, but the deep, agonizing "whys" were gone.

Later that fall, when it turned colder, I moved my favorite white wicker chair from the porch to a window in my dining room that looks out on a pond and wetland area behind my house. As I sat there one morning with Angel and my usual cup of black coffee, I began to gaze meditatively on a painting that hung there on the wall. It was a picture that once hung in Ken's office. It was not the type of painting I would normally be drawn to, but I had always liked it nonetheless and had kept it when we cleaned out his office as a memory of that time. It had been there for months, but I found myself really looking at it that day as if for the first time. And there, in the midst of a rather amorphous bunch of ground cover and flowers, was a *blue butterfly*! It had been with me all along, and I'd never seen it. I called Nancy on the spot, the only one who could possibly appreciate this as much as I did. We laughed in awed delight at this communication from Ken, our blue butterfly.

Seventh Chakra, Sacrament of Extreme Unction

In her book, Myss describes the seventh sacrament, Extreme Unction, as "receiving or bestowing the grace to finish one's unfinished business not just before death, *but as a daily part of one's life,* thus allowing a person "to love in present time." She continues, "It is the process of retrieving one's spirit from the various corners of one's life that still hold 'unfinished business'" (that "still holds juice for you," as Gwen would term i t), "or releasing regrets that continue to pull at one's consciousness . . . accepting the choices we made at the time and releasing the feeling that things could have or should have been otherwise."

When I read these words in September of 2010, I, of course, saw them as referencing all of my personal regrets around what I did or did not do, or say, or ask, during Ken's illness. I saw that releasing those regrets were paramount to moving forward in my life and to forgiving (back to the Fourth Chakra) both myself and Ken for all of the emotionally charged experiences of the previous year. But I got hung up on that. What I didn't fully understand until roughly four years later was the phrase "thus allowing a person to love in present time." Myss goes on to say, "If we fully live in the present moment, the mysteries of yesterday will gradually be unraveled for us . . . this sacrament gives us the ability to release our past experiences in order not to 'carry the dead with us.'"

As before, I had begun to write and explore what this sacrament was and what it meant to me. I had a hard time right from the start. The more I wrote, the less I understood it. This sacrament speaks to living in the present moment, to finishing unfinished business, to letting go of that which tethers us to the past, so that our spirit can become stronger than our body and our mental/emotional states. Although on some level I understood the meaning of the words, they would not slide into me, into the center of my deep understanding. Over and over again, I read from Myss's book, trying to get the words to register in some tangible way. Since "tangible" is not really a word that lends itself well to 7th chakra experience, I did my best to trust that it would all, in due time, come together.

As this was to be my last Sacrament, I wanted to include Gwen in the process. Just as I could not begin this journey without Gwen as my baptismal priestess, neither could I complete it without her presence.

When I arrived in San Diego in late September of 2010 to meet with Gwen, I was still in a muddle and was beginning to think I would never come up with anything to infuse the upcoming ceremony. Gwen and I met at Quail Gardens, a lovely botanical garden in Encinitas that both the group in earlier years and I in more recent trips had frequented with Gwen many times. Of the two areas we most enjoyed, one was a gazebo set in among some tall trees with vast expanses of bougainvillea surrounding it. The other was a large stand of numerous varieties of bamboo through which a winding path led to a lotus pond. These were our backdrops for the ceremony.

Over the next three days, we met there and had long conversations about an array of things, only some of which seemed to reflect my purpose there. Gwen's always surprising pathways to get to the heart of something did not fail here, as she guided my confused self toward some answers. This was her first admonition after I shared my frustrations: "I suggest no more rules this trip. Let the ceremony lead us. We'll find out together how to do this, and it will be fun and exciting by not knowing. Okay?"

"Okay," I replied, it totally escaping me how very 7th chakra this approach was.

The first things to show up on our quest were lizards, the tiny little lizards that comb the rocky surfaces and crevices of almost any garden in southern California. Though always there, they blend in so well with their surroundings that they are rarely even noticed. This trip, they were everywhere and very noticeable. It seemed appropriate to look at the symbolic meaning. I read about lizards in Jamie Sams's book, *Medicine Cards:* "Lizard medicine is the shadow side of reality where your dreams are reviewed before you decide to manifest them physically. This shadow can be your fears, your hopes, or the very thing you are resisting and will follow you around like an obedient dog . . . It may be time to look and see what is following along behind you." This resonated clearly with the Myss material I'd been reading.

Gwen and I talked some more about how I was tethered to the past, and more importantly, what might I be looking for in my future. Ken, of course. I yearned to connect with him more solidly, to talk with him, sense his presence, see him. Though I'd had dreams of him for sure, much of the time he didn't look like Ken, and I couldn't understand why he was withholding that experience from me. Why not appear as himself, as the Ken I loved? Gwen's thoughts came back to me as questions, geared to have me come to my own sense of it. "The answer is in the silence," I replied.

For years, Gwen had ended every meditation with a period of silence, reminding us, "For it is in the silence that Spirit speaks." As I mirrored her words back to her, I commented about all of my aching, carried on my breath within each meditation, like a prayer. She replied, "Silence speaks a thousand words, and God hears every one of them."

Then why am I hearing no answers? I thought. God and I were apparently still at an impasse.

We continued on with conversations around this theme, but I had hit a wall in my ability to comprehend my way through this sacrament. The ceremony eluded me.

Two nights before I was to go home, I had a dream. The dream itself was to prove unimportant as it stood, but it pointed the way for Gwen. In ways that were a mystery to me early on, Gwen always had the ability to turn something upside down and inside out to get someone to see a dilemma with different eyes. An inner smile emerged as she began this process with me the next morning. I told her about the dream and she had me repeat it two more times before commenting. Then she went into a now very familiar pose – left hand on her heart, right arm extended upward, shaking her hand and fingers gently back and forth down to her ear, seeming to bring information in from the ethers. I knew something special was coming. "Well," she began, "I believe we have to rewrite this dream. It will provide the statements needed for your ceremony." Together, with me writing, we developed a list of statements.

Shortly after lunch, we returned to the park in Del Mar where my baptism had taken place. We sat again at the same bench overlooking the ocean. Again, three tiny lizards scampered on a rock lying in the nearby grass to sun themselves and bear witness.

Gwen and I spoke little, simply centering ourselves and sitting quietly for a few moments. Reaching some point of knowingness, she placed her hand on my head and made a brief statement, releasing me from the past. Letting out a long, slow breath, I then read aloud the list of statements we had generated from my dream, confirming and completing the sacrament:

This Sacrament of Extreme Unction is the gateway to my future. The way I am grounded here will stay the same, but my consciousness will go to a higher level. To that end I do confirm that:

- ♥ In the future I will do lucid dreaming.

- ♥ In the future I will use what I have learned in the past to connect my chakras in a grounded heart space.

- ♥ In the future I will speak my own language by looking inward whether others understand it or not.

- ♥ In the future, my touch will tell me; I will hold my own hand in order to know my own limits.

- ♥ In the future my dark side might envelope me, may take me by surprise, but I will be able to face that darkness.

- ♥ In the future, when I am in doubt, I will call on the peaceful certainty within myself to reassure myself that I can have my cake and eat it too.

- ♥ In the future my passage will include my proper male side which attracts my welcoming female side.

- ♥ In the future I will make better use of Kundalini to nourish my 7th Chakra.

- ♥ In the future I will access my faculties as my wild child.

- ♥ In the future I will take leaps of faith with joy.

- ♥ In the future I will right what has been upset and leave no mess behind.

I've never done anything like this with a dream before or since. Gwen was indeed a magical woman of inspiration and creativity. But I admit that, although I participated as fully as I could in this sacrament, I remained unsteady before it. I could not quite take it into my heart of hearts and feel its worth. It felt scary – and what had Ken said about "scary?" It's just a word for somewhere we have never been before. And I hadn't been where those statements were taking me. I felt certain that I was not yet done with this sacrament, and those references to "in the future" underscored not only a release of the past but of the work yet to be done in order to land in that future. Yet there was hopeful anticipation of the journey.

It was not until spring 2014, more than four years after I started the sacramental journey, that I finally figured out what the Seventh Sacrament meant for me. I was sitting on my back porch enjoying the bird songs, sunshine, and spring breezes when an understanding landed on me with a nearly audible *thud*: I quickly scrawled in my journal as fast as the words came to me:

> *Here I am, still wanting to find some way to communicate with Ken more clearly, asking for access to a "next level" of our relationship, but part of me is still "back there," loving and yearning and regretting, and attaching to what was. Wanting the Ken that was. Ken isn't back there anymore. He's here, now, and he's changed since then, just as I have. And this is the only place I'm ever going to be able to connect with him again. Here. Now. The way we both are Now.*

Letting go of the past and being in the present moment was a concept I was quite familiar with, yet it had never resonated with me quite like this before; familiar, yet at the same time profound. I recalled a quote (or maybe Ken was helping me remember) by Robert Holden from his book *Be Happy*: "Sometimes in order to be happy in the present moment, you have to be willing to give up all hope for a better past." It sounded like something Ken would say, and I knew it was not the Ken of the past who could talk to me now of things beyond his knowing as a man.

Sometimes certain blessings from God come crashing in through the windows.

—Paulo Coelho, *Brida*

Ken is here now, not back there.

With that very definite knowing, I saw clearly that staying in the present with him was essential to my goal. My lingering in the romantic past, with his past self, doesn't get me there. This is the *only* place I can truly experience him, *as he is now.* The Ken of my past would always live in my heart and soul, but I truly wanted to know and experience this Ken of the present. I wanted an expansion of our relationship that only being in the present could bring. Amazingly, it was not until that moment, in 2014, that I finally completed the Seventh Sacrament.

October 18, 2010

The emotional highs of the previous few months of my journey with the sacraments were not, alas, to be completely lasting. I approached the first anniversary of Ken's death with dread. As I awoke that morning after a fitful night's sleep, I put on my armor and cast a moat around me. Although I'd done a lot of work, and the pain was not as great as a year ago, neither was it any place I wanted to go today, and I vowed to keep it at bay. However, my thoughts began to stray to that night and the dreamlike experience of those last hours with Ken. It seemed the memories would not leave me alone until I relented and let myself relive it. I told myself I didn't know what to make of it exactly. But maybe I did and just didn't want to believe what had happened. At that point I had kept those hours private, I do know there had been times when my thoughts wandered to the last few moments, and I'd wished I had followed him when I had the chance. Not wanting to actually die but wanting so very much to be with him for the voyage and perhaps catch a glimpse of what comes next. Keeping that door shut for the last year, I had been either unwilling or unable to look at the magical aura of those three hours. Even a year later, I found there were still too many wounds to heal before I had the strength to really look at *that*.

Pregnancy & Gestation – Dreaming the Book

When my original journey of the sacraments ended in the fall of 2010, I began to toy with the idea of writing about my experiences in a book. I had mentioned it a few times in my journaling but had had no real confirmation from any source that this was something I could or should do. And what exactly would I write? I was still struggling to stay afloat emotionally. How could I come to any meaningful conclusions when I was hard-pressed to understand anything in the big picture enough to write about it?

I talked about it with Gwen, telling her that all I had ever done was journal about these matters. "The content would be literally all over the place," I said.

Gwen replied, "Well, you have to know, it *will* be messy, but your journals *are* your book."

Journal entry, 11/25/2010
(date = 12/3; creativity)

Dream last night: I'm with Ken and we're pregnant! He walks with me up a small green hillside and takes me under a big white canopy where I sit on some thick, fluffy, white bedding in the shade. We are happy and excited. This is where the babies will be born. Ken offers me some fruit, pears, and I take one and bite into it. They are so juicy and flavorful. There is another person there with us, our "Helper." He throws back the gauze like curtains so we can see all directions around us. There are lots of white pillows and I lie down and stretch out my right arm under them and my hand grasps a sword that I know is to protect us. There is no fear around this; it is simply a symbolic gesture, a mother's protective nature.

After I wrote about the dream, I was drawn to pull two Runes symbolizing Ken and me – the masculine and feminine energies required for pregnancy and birth. The female position (left) was, not surprisingly, "Protection." The male position (right) was "Partnership." It was the perfect underscore for an unusual and delightful dream.

Some of the meaning seemed clear, but was there anything deeper to look at? In the dream I said "we" were pregnant, implying he is the father, partnering the pregnancy with me. Now that he was on the other side, might it be considered a sacred pregnancy? A love child born of our time together? What would that look like?

That's when I wondered whether the dream was referencing the book I'd thought about writing. Was Ken ready now to help father our book? Still, I hesitated, fearful of the commitment. I remembered Gwen asking me years earlier – when I had told her I was afraid of doing my Soul Stories intuitive work – "Is it fear? Or is it excitement? They feel very much the same, you know."

That reminder was all I needed to move forward with the idea. But what about gestation? In the dream, I was already pregnant but was not showing. If this was about the book, did birth mean the completed book? Or was birth when I start the book? After all, you have to raise a child to adulthood, right?

I set about looking for answers. And I didn't have to wait long.

Journal entry, 11/26/2010
(13/4 = foundations)

No new dream last night. I asked Ken for more info as I went to sleep, but nothing came, or at least I'm not remembering it if it happened. ☹ Wow, a hawk just landed in the tree outside my living room window. I've never seen a hawk here before and he's just perched there facing me, like he is looking in at me – not looking for breakfast! He's not moving an inch . . . how long has he been there? (checking the clock) Must be at least 6 or 7 minutes now. The Medicine Cards refer to Hawk as The Messenger; what does he want to tell me?

Journal entry, 11/27/2010
(14/5 = movement/change)

Nothing again. Maybe I just need to let it go for now. Guess I'm not supposed to know more at the moment. But I did wake up with a song stuck in my head. Where did this thing come from? Not the usual music I listen to: "565,600 minutes. How do you measure, measure a year?" From Rent, *I think. Looking back a year or forward a year?*

A LOVE STORY

Journal entry, 11/28/2010
(15/6 = nurturance of self and others)
The Hawk is back in the tree today . . .

Journal entry, 11/29/2010
(16/7 = introspection/inner work)

Dream: I'm sitting at a long table. Just me, though it feels like someone else is nearby, a man (Ken?). In front of me, almost on the opposite side of the table are several stacks of books, stacks of the same book. I am holding one of them, opened to an early page and ready to sign it, but I have no pen. At the far end of the table sits one book, different from these, all by itself. Above me floating lazily over my head is a third and different book. I feel content within this scene.

On waking, I said aloud, "OMG, Ken! This is our baby – babies! The first dream said babies! We're going to write a book – *books* – together." In a simultaneous flash I recalled Gwen telling us once that we would be working together on some kind of project one day, and we'd had no clue what she could possibly be talking about!

True to the lyrics of the song, it would be about a year before I began to assemble the thoughts and notes and messages from my dreams with my journal entries, 2010 healing journey, and other stories, to begin to develop what would eventually become this book.

From that point on, songs became Ken's favorite way to communicate with me. Sometimes a song simply came to mind, or I'd hear it on the radio, or in dreams. And the Hawk? Well, it wasn't the last time that Hawk would visit me in that same tree outside my window, and it always brought a message appropriate to my circumstances.

8

Beyond the Dark Night

My spirit guides send mentors
with their lanterns for the path
to draw me forward toward the light,
while other guides send friends or enemies
who drag their feet a step behind
to shine my old behaviors on my heels
and keep me moving on.

As 2010 came to a close, I was experiencing a rocky holiday period, again enduring the emptiness of this yearly December "love-fest" without Ken, my sarcasm and dour demeanor framing the holidays. Although I again spent time with Ken's kids, and I was so grateful to them for including me, it was a bittersweet gathering.

I had endured the 2009 holiday in a state of semi-numbness, but 2010's found me in bouts of recurring anger and well aware of it. Despite a generally uplifting journey through the sacraments, many of the healing epiphanies were still to come, and I was still in a dark place. This deeply sarcastic voice in my head kept saying I should just run away and bury myself in some unfamiliar town where I didn't have to see anyone, or go through the motions of Christmas, or the incessant playing of Christmas Carols, or all the happy holiday movies and commercials on TV. I had waited a lifetime for someone like Ken to share Christmas and so many other things with, and he was already gone. One happy Christmas was all I got?! I was back to a life of singlehood and, unlike my younger years, hating it. I had been right all along. The answer to my lifelong yearning for this loving, strong, committed, long-term relationship was No. You can't have that. But there was truly nowhere to go where I wouldn't be followed by that voice in my head, so I made the best I could of the season, all the while aching for it to just be over. It took all my focus and energy to pretend my way into the New Year, waking on January 1 with the indelible lyrics of Three Dog Night's "One Is The Loneliest Number" repeating in my brain.

All of the major steps I had taken toward healing had not marked an end to my doubts and grief and guilt. The darkness seemed to come and go like a shadow on the wall. Some days the work I'd done in 2010 was a sound support, and I remembered its lessons well. Other days, by far more numerous, I was totally disconnected, all of the hurt crashing down on me again. I was still FURIOUS at that vengeful "God."

Making Peace with God

With the welcome return of the cold, barren winter months, seemingly mirroring my soul, I turned again to my journal and my search for stability, and a bit of normalcy as well. The sadness and loneliness lingered, but eventually, thoughts arose of a future where I might resolve myself of the pain and lingering doubts about God and all the questions still unanswered.

"i beg you . . . to have patience with everything unresolved in your heart and try to love the questions themselves as if they were locked rooms or books written in a very foreign language. don't search for the answers, which could not be given you now, because you would not be able to live them. and the point is, to live everything. live the questions now. perhaps then, someday far in the future, you will gradually, without even noticing it, live your way into the answers."

—rainer maria rilke

Some months into 2011, the thaw began. It came without fanfare, or any aha moment, or a profound experience. Through countless pages of writing, and dreams, and talks with Gwen, I seemed to more or less wake up one morning and find I could actually utter the name "God" without the habitual resistance that had become lodged within.

I can only explain it as grace, because little had changed in my general attitude.

Near the Ides of March, after yet another rant at the unfairness of my plight, and finding myself at the end of the rant feeling oddly guilty for it, I heard myself murmur, "It's okay. I think He can take it." I had come, with some surprise, to a place where I could feel God's acceptance, to allow myself the anger without needing forgiveness, without needing to apologize, without being *wrong*.

Tentatively, I began to explore what I could reclaim of my beliefs about God at the time I met Ken. I admit I wasn't sure I could trust this new perspective, but as days came and went, this thaw remained. I found "God" becoming again a softer, nurturing presence. Finally, I wrote in my journal, *"I give up my war with Life. I give up my war with God."* That became a sort of mantra whenever I slipped back into my pity-party. A poem by Carl Sandburg kept repeating in my consciousness for several days after that and seemed to describe my current and ongoing process as it all was becoming more clear in my mind:

> *The fog comes*
> *on little cat feet.*
>
> *It sits looking*
> *over the harbor*
> *on silent haunches*
> *and then moves on.*

A sense of peace accompanied these lines. I realized that I'd turned a corner and was beginning to relax again with the notion of a kind and benevolent God. While all of the emotion around this consideration was not necessarily wrung out of me yet, I knew that I was, indeed, in a better place than I'd been. No fanfare, no bells and whistles, just the fog, quietly moving on, leaving me open and a bit more willing.

Contacting Ken

With this newfound release of some serious resentment, I was able to re-focus and continue my spiritual and personal quest. I attempted to seriously address the possibility of connecting with Ken in a more direct way. The craving of that connection was strong, bordering on obsession, and I devoured many books on the subject, looking for direction.

During that first half of 2011, there were several books that stood out, both discussing life after death in general and the successes some authors had had in connecting with their departed loved ones. There were also websites that offered information I was seeking. One in particular captured my attention. Most spoke of NDEs (Near Death Experiences) but one caught my attention in a major way. There was this thing I'd never heard of before, an SDE, Shared Death Experience. These were accounts of experiences had by people who were with someone they loved as that person was on his or her deathbed and somehow were able to join them at least part way to the other side.

I was jolted by these stories and could not keep myself from thinking about the night Ken died. Had this been what had happened that night? Had he some choice in those last few hours about how he left? Had the beings and the irresistible sleep been part of that? Had he orchestrated my joining him through his transition? I could barely breathe as these thoughts and questions swirled in my head, in my heart. How many times had I said we were magic, that I believed in "us" more than anything else? Yet I had been in denial then, and still was. I wanted to believe it but doubt kept me from seeing what should have been obvious.

In 2011, my focus was on getting Ken to communicate with me. Why this was, I cannot fathom now, because it's clear in retrospect that he already was. But at that point I needed *more* proof. I was insatiable for it. Along with many sessions with Gwen, I was led to have readings with two other gifted mediums as well as an exploration of Ken's and my charts with my astrologer, Paul Nunn. All three confirmed that Ken was indeed with me, seeing what I see, hearing what I hear, and always sending me messages. All I needed to do was pay attention . . . listen. . . be aware.

During one telephone session, the medium asked if I understood what two eagle feathers meant; Ken kept showing him two eagle feathers. I was at a loss. I couldn't think of any meaning for eagle feathers in my relationship to Ken. The medium suggested I keep it in the back of my mind, that something might reveal itself later. I had been sitting at my L-shaped desk, looking out the window as we talked. When I hung up the phone, I turned to face the other section of my desk, which contained cubbyholes for papers and such. My eyes fell on the farthest cubby to the left and there, propped behind boxes of paper clips and rubber bands were two eagle feathers! Ken had been right there next to me, listening to the conversation and telling this guy what he saw there at my desk: two eagle feathers. They were actually painted turkey feathers, made to look like eagle feathers that I used in some rituals on occasion. I'd forgotten they were even there. Awesome! It took my breath away to know Ken was standing right behind me.

In this same session, the medium told me that Ken wanted to do things for me; all I needed to do was ask. "He can multitask exponentially now," the medium said. "He is showing me an octopus doing something different with all eight of its tentacles." As an example, the medium mentioned that Ken was always in the car with me when I was ready to fill up the gas tank, because he knew how much the rising gas prices bugged me. Ken was helping me find the cheapest gas station around. W e never had a conversation to this effect when he was alive; gas prices were a non-issue then. But now the higher expense really annoyed me, and I was always spouting off in the car at the posted prices. No one knew that but me.

The other medium tuned in, pun intended, to Ken's and my shared love of music. Ken had been showing the medium various musical instruments. Did I know why? I told the medium about Ken's singing group, and the CDs we had made for each other for Valentine's Day. He encouraged me to pay closer attention to music of all kinds, to look for messages coming through from Ken.

Within days, music began to take on deeper meanings. Songs on the radio answered questions in my head. Or I'd wake up singing a song that I hadn't heard in years, and all day long a line or two of the lyrics repeated over and over again, clearly relevant messages Ken was sending me from beyond.

One morning after this session, I awoke with the pop song "Never Gonna Give You Up" (by Rick Astley) repeating in my head. It was the repetitive verse, you know the one, which runs periodically through the song.

I was instantly transported back to the summer of 2009. Ken had been undergoing chemo for a while at that point and often needed to rest or nap during the day. The memory, complete in its detail, surprised me with bits of information I had lost since his passing. On this particular day, while he napped, I fell into a sullen mood. I had been silently torturing myself with a series of "whys" about Ken's health. His speech was slowing, sometimes a bit slurred. Conversations were becoming shorter. Why isn't the chemo working? Why was this happening? Why does this feel so ominous? Why can't I shake this terrible feeling that I'm losing him?

Just needing to see him, touch him, I put down my chores and walked into the bedroom where I thought he was napping. Instead, I found him awake and looking at me intently as I walked in, those big baby blues capturing me in a way that made me feel seen, understood, and vulnerable. I felt like he was reading my mind. I feigned a smile as I sat down next to him. There was something in those eyes, different, "soulfull"; my heart was pounding with embarrassment at being caught in contemplation of impending doom.

"You know I'll never leave you," he stated simply and with a quiet certainty, his eyes steady, never leaving mine. His words pierced my consciousness as his eyes willed me to fully understand his meaning, to take it in on a higher level. Physically, my head was swimming a bit and I felt a little woozy during those few seconds. From that space I whispered, "I know."

I would have many reminders in the years to come of his kept promise.

For one, I was convinced that Ken was speaking to me through songs, and I began to notice it more often. At some point a few weeks into a stretch where it seemed to be happening all the time, it occurred to me that I hadn't heard any songs from Ken recently. Whimsically, I asked him if he was still there. In a humorous attempt to get me back on track, a familiar old song wafted out of the radio: "Let 'Em In" by Billy Paul. Since it sounded to me like he'd been knocking but I hadn't been letting him in, I had to acknowledge that he could be right. "Okay, okay", I jokingly responded, "I'll pay more attention from now on."

Music continues to be a reliable form of communication for us. The playful otter in Ken consistently finds the perfect lyrics to nudge me, make me laugh, and remind me that he loves me, that he's not going anywhere. He also sends wondrous answers to my queries and bewilderments. To this day I often wake up with some random song in my head and discover it's not so random after all.

Union . . . and Re-union

The solid communications through music beget a new sense of union between us. I had been looking at old pictures from Ken's life before me. Two photos particularly mesmerized me. I felt like I could easily walk into the picture and experience that moment with Ken, though we had not met then. I began to contemplate the degree to which we had felt like one, the oneness overseeing our twoness.

Shortly thereafter, I read the book *Anam Cara* by John O'Donohue. As I came to a particular passage and read it through, I was lifted into a heady state that caught me by surprise. Like many conversations about our particular magic, it spoke to the idea of our oneness and twoness. I actually have a heart-shaped rock that Ken found one day and gave to me. It was cracked nearly in half and while his words were more about "two pieces of the same heart", I see it now as mirroring the idea which O'Donohue outlines below. I tied a red ribbon around it to keep it from separating.

> *"When you find the person you love, an act of ancient recognition brings you together. It is as if millions of years before the silence of nature broke, your lover's clay and your clay lay side by side. Then in the turning of the seasons, your one clay divided and separated. You began to rise as distinct clay forms, each housing a different individuality and destiny. Without even knowing it, your secret memory mourned your loss of each other. While your clay selves wandered thousands of years through the universe, your longing for each other never faded. [This explains the experience of two souls meeting and having an instant recognition of each other.] There is an awakening between you, a sense of ancient knowing. Love opens the door of ancient recognition. You enter. You come home to each other at last. . . That which is ancient between you will mind you, shelter you, and hold you together . . . each comes out of the loneliness of exile, home to the one house of belonging. . . Each recognizes the other as the one in whom their heart could be home."*

My twenty-two months with Ken raced through my mind in a flash of words and images: "Oh, finally, it's you!" The immediate trust, immediate knowing. Oneness and twoness. The vesica-pisces. Our marriage vows. The "easy." Even an anonymous quote I'd found and used on the Memory Board at his service read, "You are the one my soul will love forever." All of this and more reiterated what I had just read, and reverberated in my bones. Was it Ken's voice who had read those words to me? No matter, the divining rod of truth rang through it, and I accepted it readily.

———— ❧ ————

Two friends, one soul.

—Euripides

———— ❧ ————

I could hardly wait to delve into this further. I asked Paul Nunn, my astrologer of over twenty years, if he could run Ken's chart and my chart and look for any commonalities. In fact, he ran charts for 2009 forward for both of us. Paul taught astrology as a continuum, as evolutionary astrology, the premise being that we continue our path even after we cross over, as we are still learning about that most recent incarnation.

In all his years of practicing and teaching astrology, having done literally thousands of charts, none of Paul's clients had ever asked for the chart of a deceased loved one. He was as fascinated as I to find out what story this might tell.

He called me excitedly to relate his discoveries. He said that Ken's and my charts had been running in parallel since before 2009. We had been doing the same cycles at the same or at nearly the same times but with one doing the negative and one doing the positive experience of those energies. Then, some months later, the same astrological pattern repeated but reversing the positive–negative aspects. On the night Ken died, October 18, 2009, we were both in the middle of the same release pattern, him doing the positive, me the negative! Remarkably, within a six-week period shortly following Ken's passing, that pattern recurred, Ken doing the negative and me the positive. Paul said we were helping each other clear a lot of mental–emotional debris through these pairings. In addition, throughout the next nearly two-year period of our charts, every time a specific astrological period peaked, it was on the 18th of the month.

I went back into my prolific journals and found amazing correspondences, showing how my experiences at the time mirrored what Ken's chart was showing, his lessons and learning continued on the other side, mirroring my own, including our changing roles and patterns, supporting each other through it. As these patterns continued over the following months and years, I was able to work with this knowledge to consciously be in sync with Ken. It was a parallel to the numerology of our names, the 18 and the 81, playing themselves out within our astrology, even though we existed on different planes. Though I have not kept up with these dual nature chartings, I have no doubt they continue to match up, and I trust we are complementing each other's work.

That Ken was here with me and communicating with me was truly a wondrous feeling. That Anam Cara experience was tangible now, and I could see through these charts and through my corresponding life experiences that we were truly connected in some way beyond the romantic, beyond what we had known in the physicality of this lifetime. Finally, something in all of this felt solid.

"What if all the things that seem so unfair turn out to make sense after all? What if every life drama we needed for the growth of our soul was provided for us?"

—Joan Borysenko

2011 continued to be a year of memories unfolding themselves from the recesses of my mind. With my anger at God in remission, I found myself finally able to look more closely at the three-and-a-half months between our marriage and Ken's death without the relentless feelings of guilt and regret that I'd tenaciously held on to for so long.

Ken's "Purrfect" Vessel

On Valentine's Day of 2012, my cat Raven passed away quite suddenly. A small blood vessel, too small in cats to be repaired, had been leaking into her lungs; it eventually took her life, and I felt I had let her suffer. Guilt – again. There had been a couple of small, telltale signs, but by the time it appeared urgent, it was too late. They could drain her lungs, but the leak would continue and the painful procedure would have to be repeated again and again. I couldn't put her through it, or myself, truth be told. I felt I had to let her go and in meditation, she told me she was ready.

Making this kind of decision for a pet is agonizing. Who am I to *decide* that she dies? She had been the most joyous and playful little kitten when I brought her home with me some twelve years before, and we had bonded so easily over toys and naps and cuddles and lap-time. How could I say goodbye to her this way? I cried on and off for days as I was thrown back into those familiar feelings of grief and guilt. Then there was Angel, who had spent nearly all her life with Raven, who was only about a year old at the time Angel came to live with us, and had mothered her as a kitten, then becoming best buddies as they grew up together. She would miss Raven too. Worst of all was the fact that they had both bonded so with Ken, and somehow saying goodbye to Raven was saying goodbye to Ken once more. The joy of the beginning and the pain of the end, yet again, and feeling raw, as death took the breath from me – again.

But when spring returned, I was compelled to look for another cat. I wanted a little older cat, closer to Angel's age, as a companion for Angel. Koko joined us that May.

Very shortly after Koko arrived, I unexpectedly had an encounter with another medium. A few minutes into our conversation she said, "You have a new cat in the household, don't you?"

"Ummm, yeah," I more or less stammered in surprise.

"This kitty has come to you for a special reason," she said. "Ken wants to be able to share physical space with you, so he has connected with Koko. She has agreed to let him 'come in' from time to time and be with you in the physical, through her. He says you'll know when it is him."

I was astonished. Dumbfounded and excited, I barely remembered anything else she had to say after that. Within a day or two, I was sitting in my usual chair watching TV one night when Koko hopped up into my lap. She turned around a few times before lowering her body into a curl on my lap, and then she slowly turned her head and tilted it up to look at me. The look on her face, that I would come to know intimately, was one of such tenderness, such love. It was Ken. I had no doubt.

I have melted under that look many times since that night, and I always respond with long strokes on her back, and rubs under the chin, which she relishes and leans into, and I sing to her in goofy lyrics that she seems to understand as our special language. Then, just as quickly, she is all Koko again, giving me a playful bite to let me know she is back.

TOBEHAPPY

Somewhere near what would have been Ken's and my third wedding anniversary (June of 2012), Brian, Ken's son, sent me a kind and lovely letter that fueled another cycle in my healing process. First, Brian reminded me of a doodle Ken frequently did:

TOB
EHA
PPY

He also shared with me that he knew I had made Ken very happy and how appreciative he was that his dad had been able to experience that before he died. The letter brought me to tears and probably an over-effusive 110 reply to Brian, but it also brought me to a creative endeavor that allowed me to really delve into what this doodle of Ken's meant to him and what it had to teach me. I became possessed. For days I created paintings of this TOBEHAPPY doodle in various colors and formats, then made four of them into note cards. I gave sets of them as Christmas gifts that year to friends and family. I included a quote on the back of the card that Brian had shared with me, an approximation of something Ken had said to him once:

> "My mission in life is to be happy. To be happy requires me to be true to myself, which means focusing on those things in life that bring me a sense of inner fulfillment and pleasure. And if I can be consistent in that focus, I will be a blessing to others, especially to those I love."
>
> —Kenneth King

In the process of doing the artwork for the cards, and in going over Ken's statement dozens of times in my head, I could see that the past was never going to change no matter how much I wished it to do so, nor could I ever go back. How well I knew this to be true in my head, but my heart was another matter. I had been living as though the past was reality and that I could stop time somehow if I held on tight enough to that hope, and lived in the memories. And by that I was robbing myself of a happy true present, of being any kind of blessing to anyone, including myself. I knew I had to give that up and be happy in the now, happy in the presence of what I had, not mired in what I had lost.

As if in affirmation of that sentiment, I watched a music documentary the evening after I picked up the cards from the printer, and the first song bursting out of the TV? "Pack up your troubles c'mon get happy. . ."

9

Transitions

Cut loose from bondage,
some of it self-inflicted,
she licked her wounds . . .

Then, crawling inward,
began to see things inside out,
herself included.

From this position
she looked at her world again,
decided
she would peel the layers of herself
with gentleness,
allow herself to know
this time
she holds the key to all her bindings.

The 2012 holidays came and went with comparative ease. I was finally able to enjoy them again without the morose emotions of the last three years. Holiday time spent with my friends and the Kings, my new family, was nourishing and supportive.

I'd been in touch with Gwen, and we spoke some about her prediction of the date of her transition, a prediction she made some twenty years before: March 26, 2013. That date was not far away, and she was on my mind a lot. When we talked of it, she related several dreams to me with symbolism rampant of crossing from one place to another, places vastly different from each other. Gwen seemed unbothered by the prospect, and I felt assured that since she had been preparing for the day for many years now, she carried no particular hesitation to experience the event to come.

However, it made me nervous, anxious, and unbalanced. I joined two other friends and longtime followers of Gwen's work for what turned out to be a final visit to see her. We left on Christmas Day 2012 and returned on New Year's Day 2013. As always, it was a gift to be with her, but I returned with a hollow feeling in the pit of my stomach and a more-than-usual ache in my heart at leaving her.

Gwen's Transition

On February 26, 2013, I woke with a fleeting dream that dissolved into the light as soon as my eyes opened. It left a disconcerting feeling I could not identify, but I later realized it was exactly one month before the date Gwen had picked for her death. Was she right? Was that dreaded day really so close? Would I soon lose her too? All day I lingered in a lonely quiet that would not abate.

I found myself sitting on the couch crying for all the people I'd lost, crying for Gwen, though her voice was still but a phone call away. I opened the door of the microwave and found my mug with yesterday's coffee still in it. Somehow that seemed so very sad, like a time capsule to remind me that what was invigorating can easily turn cold and bitter. I drew a Rune: "Uruz" – Strength, the Rune of terminations and new beginnings.

I called Gwen late that afternoon and we talked a little about the Rune and the coming date, and I eventually asked what had been lingering on the tip of my tongue all day. "Do you want me to come? . . . in March?"

She sounded a bit far away when she said, "Thank you, but I don't think so. Not now anyway. It's enough that you are willing."

We said our "I love yous" as we always did, but I continued to be out of sorts, a nervous anxiety seeping into my bones. Bedtime came on much the same note, and I worked my way into sleep, hoping to meet up with her in the dreamtime.

On March 3, I called Gwen to chat as we usually did once or twice a week. She didn't answer, but I left a message. She never called back. At the very end of our Gatherings, all holding hands around the circle, Gwen would routinely ask us to very slowly let go of each other's hands before saying goodbye, so no one would feel abandoned. The last of this ritual had begun.

A LOVE STORY

On March 5, I was up early for some reason. I'd been restless all night, waking several times before finally giving up around five a.m. I got out of bed, made some coffee, and sat looking out at the wetland area behind my home. It was a peaceful scene, as always, especially in the quiet of the early morning hours, and it readily put me in a meditative space. I sat there fingering the Runes, and I finally pulled out "Ansuz" – Signals, the messenger rune. A tingle went up my spine.

I gazed out my window and saw that hundreds of crows had gathered in the treetops behind the pond, random groups of them taking off and landing in large numbers. When had they all arrived? When I walked into the living room to get my journal, I heard the clear and raucous voice of a crow reverberating down the chimney into the fireplace, as though making some personal announcement to me.

When the phone rang, I noticed the 858 area code and thought, "Oh maybe that's Gwen calling me back." In the same instant I realized the number was not Gwen's. I answered, and it was Joan, Gwen's daughter. She was gone. I knew it as soon as Joan identified herself. Gwen was gone.

Doing my best to comfort Joan, I listened to the details as she spoke through sniffles. Joan's brother, who had been staying with Gwen, had taken her to the hospital the day before. She had not been feeling well and had asked him to take her. At the hospital it was confirmed that she had a bad case of pneumonia, that it would be a bit of a long road but that, with a treatment regimen, they could get her healthy again. In true Gwen fashion – I could actually hear her voice saying the words – she had replied, "Ohhh, no. Just keep me comfortable and let me go." And then, exactly three weeks prior to the date she, and all of us, had been living with for years, she quietly passed.

After the phone call I settled into a strange cocoon. It felt as though I was merely looking on into this life event that belonged to someone else. I was calm, centered and remarkably peaceful. Somewhere within that "looking on" I recall being aware of how very differently this was affecting me compared to the hours following Ken's death. This was not a numbing experience but an oddly expansive one, and I knew it would continue in this vein – no dark night this time.

"I'm cherishing the bravery
with which you let me go.
You hold me in your heart
with open hand."

— Gwenana, "Farewell Blessing" from *Ordinary Wisdom*

How odd, I pondered, that this woman I loved so dearly would not generate at least as much pain with her passing as my beloved Kenneth. Within the blink of an eye, I was made aware of how much and in what wondrous ways I had been healing over these past three years, how much Gwen had offered me of herself over the past twenty-plus years and even more so since the deaths of our husbands. She had prepared me and others well for her passing, given us a solid foundation of spiritual support and understanding that left me certain that she was not "gone" at all. How interesting that I came to this realization so quickly, and immediately seeing all the stepping stones behind me that had led me to this place.

I made the phone calls to share the news of Gwen's passing with my Gateways sisters. After that, a few soft, gentle tears fell quietly and effortlessly down my cheeks. I settled into the silence. As Gwen would often say, "The air was thick with Spirit." It was the same thickness I had felt the night Ken died, almost gelatinous at times, and remained so for the rest of the day. I relaxed contentedly into that cocoon, feeling Gwen's presence everywhere.

That night, exactly twenty-four hours after Gwen's death, I awoke abruptly and could not get back to sleep. All my teachers who had ever made a serious impact on me from throughout my life were, one by one, parading through my mind. I drifted in and out of that scene a few times. And then, on that border between asleep and awake, through the mists of this 'tween time, came Gwen, easily and clearly visible. I could feel her presence. At first, I saw there were some unusual images, mostly shapes – just triangles and circles (much like those on the cover of her first book of poetry, *Ordinary Wisdom*), and taking on the appearance of various items . . . books, pictures, pottery, and well, just shapes. I had a clear sense that these images represented our past lives together. Next, I saw Gwen lying in her bed, eyes closed, with me standing next to her. I leaned over to kiss her forehead. Though our bodies were visually present, my body sort of went through hers as I kissed her. Last, in dream state, I appeared asleep in *my* bed and she, standing next to me, gently touched my shoulder and stroked my hair. She was dressed in the beautiful goddess gear she often wore at her Heartseek Gatherings.

I awoke gently, awestruck at the grace that had brought us together in this way, that had prevented the physical miles between us from keeping us from saying goodbye before this lifetime, too, became another circle or triangle spent together on this earth.

"Look for me in the place between sleep and awake. There I will always love you. There is where I'll be waiting."

— Tinkerbell, from the movie *Hook*

I leapt from my bed and went straight to the Runes. I blurted out a question imprinted on my heart: "Oh, Mom, where are you?" A Rune practically adhered itself to my hand: "Laguz" – Flow.

Then I asked, "Where am I?" and the Rune that nearly flew into my fingertips was "Wunjo" – Joy. Gwen still knew how to turn a situation upside down with a single word!

One more question: "How are you?" I felt a need to meditate into this question, so I turned to the Soundscapes channel for some music. These were the first three songs:

"Through the Veils" by Unita"
17 Seconds to Anywhere" by Liz Story
"And Rest" (from an album named *Sun Down, Moon Up*)

It felt like Gwen was telling me the story of her passage so beautifully it would seem to need no further words. I found myself chuckling at the perfection of how this had been playing out. Her presence was still so strong and her life not at all lost, still accessible, still with me – here, now. "What an extraordinary woman," I said to myself with no small degree of fascination, and no need to use the past tense. My experiences with Gwen went on rather continuously for the entire month and well into the next before they tapered off into more occasional, yet regular, visits.

At the end of March I felt called to go to San Diego, remembering she had said "not right now" when I'd asked if I should come. I went to all of our usual places and felt her everywhere. I'd also been in touch with her son, Karl, who had taken her to the hospital. He was helping clear out the house, and many of Gwen's things were to go to some of her "flock." I went to the house to pick up those items that were coming back to Michigan. Karl and I talked for quite some time about her. It was clear to me how much he honored this person who was not only "Mom" but also the woman known as Gwen and Gwenana, a spiritual mentor to so many. He seemed to understand these personas as one and the same and held great love and affection for both.

Two days before I left San Diego, I shipped home the items from Gwen that would be shared with my spiritual sisters, who had, of course, all been dealing with their own journeys following Gwen's passing. Among those items, I had somehow ended up with another rather large, heart-shaped stone. It seemed unlikely that I should either pack it or ship it and I pondered what to do with it.

The next morning, my last day in the area, I took it to Torrey Pines State Park, one of Gwen's favorite places, that sits perched high over the Pacific Ocean near Del Mar. I stopped and walked the beach below, where she had gathered stones worn smooth by the ocean which she transformed into Rune Stones countless times before. Then I drove up the winding, narrow road to the top and parked near a spot that had been a favorite of Gwen's. With the stone in my hands, I sat on a bench Gwen and I had shared on many occasions drinking in the scenery opening out in front of me. I looked down at the road, watching the cars below that looked like ants at a picnic. People on the beach looked even smaller, and the ocean stretched out into infinity, touching the sky at the horizon, and, I imagined, rolling like Niagara off the ends of the earth. Ken must have been there too, as strains of "On A Clear Day" crooned in my head. I loved this place too, maybe as much as she did. I felt her standing there next to me breathing deeply, as I did now.

A LOVE STORY

"Grieve not.
For I am still at your side, laced through your ribs,
Reaching for your heart."

—Susan Mrosek, *The Pondering Pool*

————— ✦✦✦ —————

I took the heart-shaped stone, made up a short ceremony as I went along, drew a couple of Runes, and after giving it a big kiss, placed the stone there, kneeling to hide it among some bushes for protection. I said a few words of farewell and, reluctantly, left the park.

Later that day, in a favorite store in Encinitas, I found a small stone, a bright red heart. It sits on my alter today, always connecting me to that piece of Gwen's heart I left behind.

Bring On the Laughter

On July 4, 2013 (Independence Day), I had an attack of pancreatitis brought on by my gall bladder. I was in the hospital for a week, and about a month later, I had my gall bladder removed. If you have read any of Louise Hay's work, you may recall that the pancreas and gall bladder have to do with anger, bitterness, hard thoughts, and a loss of belief in the sweetness of life. These maladies were my body's way of expressing all the hard emotions I had stored there for so long. While I had made progress in releasing all that, the experience was a reminder to continue those efforts in all seriousness and to stop once and for all that once habitual behavior and instead embrace the philosophy of "TOBEHAPPY."

A lovely event gave me a head start in that direction. Early in October, 2013, I had Ken's daughter Stephanie, and her husband, Kevin, over for dinner. I had been doing that with some regularity, enjoying their company and hearing about their lives. Ken seemed very present that day as I prepared the meal, perhaps more so than usual before these dinners. I thought it was because it was his birthday. At dinner, we chatted over a nice meal, but before we were about to get up from the table, there was a pause, a pregnant pause as it turned out. Stephanie would be having a baby in the spring!

Giddy happiness sprang into our conversation. When I queried if they had thought about names, they confirmed that, if they had a boy, they would name him Kenneth Robert – for Ken, of course, and for Kevin's Dad, Bob. Ken stood just behind me, grinning like any expectant grandpa would.

It was during that period of time that the idea of our writing our book returned to the forefront. It seemed time to get started in earnest. With that came the inevitable doubts that rise with nearly any creative endeavor.

All of the "what ifs" buried in my long list of fears bubbled up into several questions. Can you *commit* to writing this book with some level of honesty? Can you really put down on paper for others to read, what is written in the sanctuary of your own heart? Are you willing to share that to the best of your ability and then let it go out into the world on its own?

I decided I had to prove to myself that I could, so I committed, starting January 1, 2014, to do a weekly blog for one year. Through the course of that year, I found I did have a well of ideas to dip into and was led into a variety of topics, humorous and serious, whimsical and thoughtful, and began to show myself out loud. I discovered a thirst for exploring my writing style. I began to find my voice as a writer and came to trust that if I just sat down and started, good, bad, or indifferent, something would always come to the page. I had fun. And for the first time in years I had a purpose.

The Hawk Speaks

In November 2014, I did not see the hawk that had visited me every November since Ken died. Usually, he would sit on a low branch (not a particularly hawk-like trait) and face my front window, looking directly in at me as I looked back at him, staying there for several minutes without moving. I always felt that it was Ken coming to check in on me, to let me know he was around and watching over me. When I didn't see him in 2014, it made me sad. I felt a loss. Doubt washed over me as I wondered again if Ken was moving on in some way.

Then, on January 4, 2015 (seven years to the day since I first met Ken), the hawk showed up in the tree. I was happy to see him, and I naturally wondered what message he had for me. Given that particular day, I was certain it would be an important one.

"Grief isn't just something to endure; . . .
"We must explore it with curiosity and patience and we
must allow it to stay in
our hearts until it is ready to leave."
—Mary Pipher, *Women Rowing North*

The next day I saw a huge pile of feathers on the ground just under the branch where the hawk always sat. They were the feathers of a mourning dove, who are typically ground feeders, and therefore easy prey. Surely, the hawk had killed the mourning dove, a sweet bird that has for many years been a totem of mine. I love their calm, sweet song at dawn and dusk. My pain was immediate; it struck my heart with surprising force. The hawk that I loved and admired, that I thought of as Ken, had killed a beautiful mourning dove? It hurt, felt like a betrayal. What am I supposed to do with that? What am I to make of this message?

In some cultures, seen or heard in a certain way, the song of the mourning dove portends a death – hence the name of the bird. Was Ken saying goodbye? Was the fear I'd held all along that he would leave me coming true? Was this the end of his promise to never leave me? I pondered this dismal scenario over the next few days. And then, with the suddenness of epiphany, I understood. Gwen's voice echoed in my head. Her wondrous ability to turn anything upside down to look at what had been hidden gave me the obvious answer: My initial view melted away as I saw that instead of mourning a "final death," a final goodbye, the hawk had proclaimed *the death of mourning*. Ken was not sending me a baleful message, or saying goodbye in any way. He was saying, "The time for the death of mourning has come. Don't mourn me any longer. You are free. Your Spirit is free. And so is mine."

10

The Power of Love

And as we part and join
and join and part
our hearts are blended
like the taffy on its pull.
And thick and strong and beautiful
becomes the braided ribbon
of our lives.

Only a week after Ken and I first met, he invited me to his house to watch a movie. When I got there, he explained that there was a specific movie he wanted to share with me; it was a film that was important to him on many levels and it resonated strongly as a kind of love he'd always wanted to experience. It was the Robin Williams film *What Dreams May Come*, which, though a Williams fan, I'd never seen before. We settled in on the sofa, and I was nestled up against Ken with his arms around me, his chin resting lightly on the top of my head. We hardly moved or spoke, both of us entranced by the story unfolding on the screen.

Williams's character, Chris, and his wife, Annie, are soul mates. They are living a fulfilling, married life when Chris unexpectedly dies. Annie is bereft at losing him, becomes deeply depressed, and eventually commits suicide. Chris watches from "heaven," unable to reach her, to save her, despite his many tries. When Chris is told that Annie will not be joining him in heaven because of the darkness surrounding her death, Chris won't accept that. As the movie description summarizes: "When they met they were conjoined as soul mates in a divine love to exist no longer as two, but as one. (With) a love so powerful it defies the bounds of heaven . . . Chris journeys to the very depths of the underworld to save her . . . and he does."

131

At the time, it was wondrously romantic but also a deeply metaphysical look at love. The notion that soul mates exist and that connection continues after death is powerful. Ken and I talked about this story many times over the next two years. It became a touchstone in the exploration of our seemingly magical relationship. And that was before we had any idea that Ken would soon die.

I watched the film again recently, and I was overcome by the parallels between the movie's love story and the story of Ken and me. Granted, and thank you God, my depression and anger and resentment were nothing like the scope of Annie's, but I had been in a state of extreme dark emotion without Ken, with no "up" in sight. The only thing I trusted was him, and us. And time and again, he came through: with dreams, with songs, with whispered encouragements of all kinds. He showed up; he crossed the veil to bring me back to our love, to what love can do in the darkest of times. Indeed, as I write this last line, as if Ken is sending confirmation, I'm hearing Huey Lewis's voice in my head belting out "The Power of Love"!

Inertia

Yet, dark times could still get the best of me, even after years of effort, and I began to notice a lethargy creeping in occasionally. I tried to pretend all was well in my day-to-day existence of running errands, attending social engagements with friends or family, or setting up the usual appointments. But my mind kept whispering the famous, mythical words of Greta Garbo: "I want to be alone."

With the completion of 2014 and the successful completion of my blog, I hit a wall. The entirety of the scope of writing a book came at me in waves and washed away any sense I'd had of how this process might look. I told myself I was just "in the throes of" writing which, according to Word Detective, is an old English phrase meaning to twist, turn, or writhe; an agonizing struggle. It certainly seemed appropriate to my situation.

As I slowed from near stop to full stop and lingered there, I found it harder and harder to get back to the page. It had to do with what I had been calling solitude in my journals but what now appeared to be a total life inertia.

I noticed how many projects and tasks had been on my to-do list for a long time, how little I accomplished in any given day. How little real fun I had anymore. How little I laughed. I was quick with excuses for not doing tasks and projects; for not having people over or joining some activity or group outing. I would promise myself "next time," but next time never happened. I was also trying to write, but I kept getting stuck, kept walking away from the "baby" that I still believed Ken and I were bound to create together. It seemed I was always saying I "have no time." I followed ingrained habits to start the day, auto-piloted through the middle, and was too tired at night.

I wasn't letting life in, or moving towards it. In short, I had lost my drive "ToBeHappy." Inertia held me captive.

"We tend to seek captivity because we are used to seeing freedom as something that has neither frontiers nor responsibilities."

—Paulo Coelho, *Life: Selected Quotations by Paulo Coelho*

Inertia is deadly. It creeps in, unnoticed. At first, it seems like a practice of solitude and quiet that allows for centering and balance. Then one day, you realize you're in a rut, that the calm you needed to survive has become a prison of your own making. When inertia set in for me, I discovered, with disappointment, that after years of grieving, healing, and finally celebrating my past and present life with Ken, I still had more inner work to do.

I came to realize that I was trying to protect myself from unknown threats from "out there" where there was no safety. I wanted to believe that if I stayed very still and quiet, somehow the gods would not see me, would not wreak havoc on me again. Like a rabbit, frozen in the presence of a predator, I hoped I would not be noticed. Safety. Back to my recent Baptism sacrament. What had I said? That I would trust in my safety by the Grace of Spirit? It seemed I was being tested on my vow.

Where had this come from? I had always been a fairly positive person; how had I come to this pessimism? Had I somehow trained myself to fear, to believe that I was powerless? Recalling again the lyrics of *Amazing Grace* that I had sung to Ken, I took a deep breath and heard what could have been my baptismal song, Ken singing it back to me now. *"Through many dangers, toils and snares, I have already come. Tis Grace that's brought me safe thus far, and Grace will lead me home."*

I could see what was going on now, knew it intellectually, and I thought that once I had this awareness, the inertia would fall away naturally, fairly easily. But the nature of inertia is that it's hard to get moving again.

What I eventually found was that these stops and starts were blessings in disguise, each stopping point leading to another insight that was integral to what I needed to address in my own healing process, and thus, in turn, integral to the completion of our book.

During this particular period of inertia, I began to doubt the trust I had in the "us" of Ken and me. I tried to look honestly at my unceasing belief that Ken and I are magic, that we had and have some special link that few others do. Was it truth? Or was it an ego boost for a once-deflated heart that could not face the loss? I remembered with a chuckle something Ken often said: "The truth will set you free, but first it will make you miserable."

Every relationship is special, after all. Every relationship appears in our life for a reason. Every relationship is here to open our heart in some way. That was a truth I still believed. So I began to explore the "what ifs" while trying not to flinch: What if he had not died? What if we had then discovered that we weren't so magical? What if I'd made this all up in an effort to hang on to the perfection of what we had shared during our short time together?

These thoughts haunted me. I knew I had to come to terms with the possibility that I'd put Ken and our relationship on some sort of pedestal, on an altar of love that could never have held up over time. Everything I'd believed about us now stood in a shadow. Had the truth eluded me all along? Had we merely been two lost people who fell in love and whose relationship had come to a tragic end? Could it all possibly have been as basic as that? These questions made me miserable.

Upon much reflection, many meditations, and other tools of the heart, I found the courage to consider, and deeply feel, several other scenarios that might have occurred had Ken not died. Each conveyed all the disappointment, all the frustration, all the regret and guilt, and all the fear and anger and grief for what had been and what had been lost, again. Among these were:

- ♥ We both fall into our same old patterns and make the same old mistakes, and end up staying together out of habit but resenting each other for the rest of our lives.

- ♥ We come to those same resentments again, but give up, and endure yet another divorce and more disillusionment.

- ♥ We battle through the challenges that inevitably befall any marriage and come to a shared acceptance of each other and a certain level of contentment, dull but comfortable like an old pair of shoes.

- ♥ Ken gets cancer, goes through treatment and survives, his mind and/or personality are irrevocably changed, and he becomes a different person from the man I fell in love with.

While these scenarios were all painful in their own way to consider, by looking them squarely in the face, they lost their power, and helped me return to trusting my heart. What I've chosen to believe instead is the picture that seemed to be unfolding during the short but meaningful twenty-two months that we had together. If Ken had lived, I believe wholeheartedly that we would have maintained our commitment to doing things differently after learning from our past. Through all the challenges of a long-term relationship, we would have found our way, retained the magic, relied on each other through whatever came our way, stayed solid in the love that birthed "Us" and never lost sight of how lucky we were to have found each other. The romance intact, I like to picture us still holding hands into dotter-hood, gaga in love, and always grateful for each other. It was the very picture of what I had always imagined "true love" to look like. I ran across a quote long before I ever met Ken, likely decades ago, that struck me even then as what, from childhood, has always been my longing for this kind of love:

"the first of all my dreams
was of a lover and his only love
strolling slowly (mind in mind)
through some green, mysterious land . . ."

—e. e. cummings

The truth, of course, is that I'll never know – not in this lifetime anyway. As James Twyman quotes a Swami saying in *The Kabbalah Code*, "There is nothing to solve, and you'll never understand it. You are trying too much with your mind, but it's not your mind that has brought you this far – it's your soul." Perhaps there are parallel universes where all these other possibilities have played out. But with no one able to contradict me, why not carry forward this most positive and romantic vision? Why not have complete faith in Gwen's statement, "What is once joined in love can never be parted"? My experiences over these last years leave no doubt in my mind that Ken has kept his promise: "You know I'll never leave you."

Are we truly Anam Cara? Is our relationship something mystical, spanning all time and space? It is, I suppose, a romantic notion that may, or may not, be true. I choose to believe that it is because, first of all, I am a hopeless romantic at heart. And it's true because I want it to be true. Does that make it any more or less valid? You'll have to make up your own mind about that. But as for me, I do believe. I believe because it is in my DNA to do so. I believe because the course of events since January 4, 2008, lead me in no other direction. I believe because all I really have is belief. Perhaps it is all any of us have in the end, belief in something greater than us, belief in the power of that force, belief that anything is possible, belief in what love is capable of no matter which side of the veil we are standing behind, whether you can see your Beloved/beloved or not. Though tenuous and frail as it can feel, belief is the sinew of the soul.

I am left then with some reflections on the bigger picture, on my bigger picture, by accepting my experiences as kernels of truth with which I can now move forward more easily, living and enjoying my life, welcoming whatever the future holds while being comfortable with the intangible, with a level of not knowing.

A LOVE STORY

———⊶⊷⊷———

"Some stories don't have a clear beginning, middle, and end. Life is about not knowing, having to change, taking the moment and making the best of it, without knowing what's going to happen next. Delicious ambiguity. . ."

—Gilda Radner

———⊶⊷⊷———

We talk about the veil, but as Carolyn Myss says, "There is no veil." The strength of love is the reason for that. Sight is not the only way to experience a departed loved one. Neither is sound or touch. It is love that brings us closer, love that enables a person we miss to whisper to us in dreams or meditations, or through nature's messengers, or through music, chance encounters, books, quotes, movies, TV commercials . . . literally *anywhere, anytime.* In fact, I believe it is when we are least focused on an issue that the message shows up in some form we may not be expecting. When we ask and go on about our business while waiting for a response, we get out of our own way; we drop our cerebral barriers and stop *thinking* our way to an answer. We are then more likely to relax into our other senses and allow them to speak to us.

We need only keep our awareness sharp to figure out just how they are managing to communicate with us. Once we determine that method, it becomes easier to notice the messages. Our loved ones want to communicate with us, but we have to help; in fact, we need to tell them when we see "it" and want more of "that." They *will* respond once they know we are hearing them. They are right here with us always; they see us, hear us, answer us in whatever way *we* are able to see, hear, experience. This I know for sure.

Ken, clearly, has chosen mostly nature, music, numbers, and dreams to communicate with me, because these are things we shared in life and had in common from the start. We had already used these languages to communicate, and thus they were the easiest to utilize across planes. Ken knew I would pay attention to those things naturally, and once I was able to release my mentalizing, I could see that, and I made sure to confirm that to him.

After I had experienced this form of communication a few times, I realized I could ask questions and get answers from him. I put out an intention and waited for a reply. I like to think of it as a form of "e-mail" – energetic mail. Amusingly, it's the way we began our relationship and the way we continue it now. Today, my conversations with Ken are not always big splashy "ooo, ah, wow" moments. They're more like the everyday, living-with-someone conversations, quite comforting actually in their "everydayness." Sometimes I don't even have to ask a question to elicit a response.

For example, one day not long ago, I was having difficulty with a mundane chore, and I was feeling overwhelmed and rushed and irritated. As usual, the TV was turned to the Music Channel, so songs were playing randomly as I worked. In the midst of my frustration, two short lines stood out from a song that I found out later was Willie Nelson's "Just Breathe" and made me stop in my tracks. Pretty much a reiteration of the title of the song, I was told to stay present and, well, just breathe!

When I heard the message, I had to chuckle. Taking that deep breath and recognizing Ken was chiming in with some unrequested advice, I asked if there was anything else he wanted to tell me. My eyes immediately rested on my Runes, easily within reach. I drew one, and the basic message was, "We do without doing and everything gets done." I had to admit he was right. I slowed way down, skipped the attempted shortcuts, and followed through with my tasks in a mindful way. Before I knew it, I was done and onto something more enjoyable.

The Experience

Humor can often open us to a larger view of something, and hearing the admonishment to just breathe (also something Gwen frequently said), even as it brought me laughter, also brought me to something important about our evolving relationship. For perhaps the first time, Ken had sent me a song that I was unfamiliar with. That had intrigued me, and once freed up from the task at hand, I found my way to the computer to look up the song. The lyrics repeated the admonishment about breathing several times and, at one point, spoke of "loving you" and seeing each other on the other side. Through that line, I was brought to yet another "full circle moment."

Not only did the words remind me of Gwen, the words "just breathe" meant something else to me as well. As I fell into reverie yet again, I was taken back to the night Ken died, when I was holding his hand and willing him to just breathe. Now, all these years later, coming to the end of writing our book, I realized I hadn't really related my take, at this point, on the mysteries of that all-important night. I had certainly come to some serious "what if" kinds of inner questioning but hadn't bought the T-shirt yet. I had intended to get back to it, alluded to it in some of my thoughts, but as all the chapters have come and gone, I have always managed to pretty much side-step any final resolution around that night. Why?

How do I begin to get a handle on that *Experience* in any way that would clarify things for myself as well as offer you some explanation of what I've felt about that night? Clearly it provided the major conduit for writing this book, but just as clearly, it has affected me deeply and impacted my soul's journey in this lifetime. It holds a certain kind of magic within it, of course, and I've often said Ken and I are magic. But the night he died, the magic died too . . . for a while. I couldn't look at his death, so I couldn't look at the manner of his passing. I knew it had been a gift, but I couldn't accept his death as "gift" in any way. So I couldn't take in my experience of that night in its enormity for a very long time and, therefore, couldn't even share it with anyone.

The magic, however, was still there waiting for me, and when I was finally able to go back to that night, to go within and be there again, I found I could still FEEL it in my body. I could still see The Tall One, feel the thickness of the air and the warmth, fall into the pull of sleep despite my desire to stay awake, sense the energy and the fullness of the space around us, "see" the whoosh at the end and know the return to the heaviness of the ordinary world and to our measure of time, my head swimming with it all.

I've always known that *he* was all right, that he was safe and content, melting into that Oneness we had so often discussed. It was me who was wounded, broken, and hurting. I hadn't needed *The Experience* to assure me of *his* state of being but to support me through my own, through the deeply painful and unrelenting feeling of loss. It was only later that I began to consider that the gift in it was, for me, a confirmation of the grace and Love we are offered when Death comes, the union (or re-union) with that Love, and the true power of Love.

For me, Gwen's words, "What is once joined in love can never be parted," always had to do with love in the physical world, karmic relationships, etc. For example, I'd always looked at my first marriage and saw that the love I had felt for him would always be there and his for me. You can't not have loved someone then, just because you don't love them now. In that sense, that love will always be there. But I'd never really considered that love goes on after someone dies. Sure, I knew I had loved my parents and they had loved me. I have memories of that love; I miss them; I still love them . . . but somehow I hadn't quite connected the dots that they still loved me! Incredible. Why would I ever have thought that once your physical life is over, you are devoid of that emotion and just stop loving who you loved? That's how Anam Cara works – you *remember each other*, your connection, your love. When it finally hit me, I truly understood the *magic* of love and how it crosses all time and space. Being allowed a glimpse into Ken's passing was proof of that.

I do believe I had a Shared Death Experience that night. Remembering how different everything felt, I knew I had been held in "sacred time" where what was happening here on earth was held in abeyance while I was allowed to participate in something beyond my comprehension. It was for me, in every sense, a mystical experience, one that try as I have, remains ineffable; words have never been able to capture what I felt, what I was part of. I realize that at some unnoticed point between then and now, I have embraced the fullness of it and hold it dearly in my heart as a kind of proof that the God I have agonized over for so long, was so angry with, never left me, just as Ken has never left me.

I remembered telling Ken prior to his passing that I wanted to be with him, to be holding his hand when he left. Ken communicated to me recently, in meditation, that despite the fog of the narcotics and the intensity of those moments, he knew he wanted that too. Though earlier on I questioned the validity of what I thought might have been an SDE, I no longer doubt. A knowing has replaced that doubt; it was as real and tangible an experience as I've ever had. Ken and his helpers negotiated my consciousness so that I might actually be "present" to the process and be standing behind the veil with him for a scant moment in time. Death is a sacred transition, and I was welcomed, with some brief exceptions when sleep was induced, to share that ceremony with him. It has left me with no real fear of death as well as a conscious awareness of life being a continuum. From past lives to current, parallel, and future,

I have one soul that journeys through all of them. And that one soul is a part of The One that travels with me always.

I am reminded of the part in my wedding vows that spoke of the vesica pisces. Within the center, the eye, of the vesica pisces is Love and Union. Love and Union between people, within relationships . . . and always with Spirit, because God, Yahweh, Buddha, Allah, Universe, by whatever name you call this energy, IS Love, ever present Love. Therefore, nothing said or done in love can ever be without Spirit. God's Love, expressed as Grace, was provided to allow my SDE with Ken. And so, God is ever present within the vesica pisces of Ken and Gloria. Even if my beloved is no longer in physical form, we are still together because Love is still present, and "what is once joined in Love can never be parted." I have the availability of that shared space, shared with God, shared with my Soul, shared with Ken, because God has been with me from before my first breath.

". . . it is the act of being met where we are that enables us to let God in. Nothing more or less . . . The ascent to heaven is inward. The dove in downward flight is the symbol of that communion . . . It is the symbol of the love and light of God – a love that never destroys and always connects. We do not have to be good or follow imaginary rules in order to qualify for that love; it is not a matter of us deserving it or having to earn it. . . We need only recognize that the dove is not on its way; it has already arrived."

—Roseanne Farano, *The Dove in Downward Flight*

The Grace and Love of God that was necessary for *The Experience* to happen is a truth that I must accept, because Love is Love, the ultimate Oneness within the Twoness of our existence, so if I believed in Ken's love for me then I could not deny God's love for me as well. To this day, I feel a deep sense of awe at the privilege I was given, this precious gift from Ken, and from Spirit. As I write these paragraphs, I recall the anger as I railed against this same God some ten years ago, and my certainty that I would never trust "Him" again. But human certainty is, I suspect, a great cosmic joke, and God loves a good laugh.

Has this experience solidified my picture of God? Yes . . . No . . . Somewhat. My belief is that God shifts and evolves as I shift and evolve, as we all do, an ever Evolving Essence, just as I am. Since I am a part of the oneness within the twoness within the Oneness, I nourish God's evolution, just as God nourishes mine. We share our own vesica pisces if you will, and just as in any relationship, we change each other, hopefully for the better.

Aside from Love itself, CHOICE and CHANGE are really the only constants; they are, in every sense, Universal, as is the Love that fuels them. We have opportunities every day to choose what and how we move through our experiences. And through choice, change happens; we evolve and will never again be the person we were yesterday. God walks that path with us, but not for us.

"Perhaps it is not God's job to decide what actually happens in our daily lives, but to be there to guide us, especially when things go terribly wrong . . . to help us find whatever it is that will heal us and bring us back to joy."

—Unknown

I have returned to a belief in Spirit, not as a vengeful male presence meting out rewards and punishments, but as the creative force of the Universe, the complex and perfect order of Nature, with both masculine and feminine qualities: *They*, rather than He or She. God is Divine Energy in motion, constantly changing. God is not the Puppeteer, planning my life and alternately wreaking havoc on me or favoring me with wondrous gifts, but lives *in* me, expressing *through* me by my free will and my ability to surrender to Love. Free will and a surrender to

A LOVE STORY

Love are often at odds in this world. I know that is true within me. It's a messy duality, as anyone can see by just watching the evening news or looking in the mirror. But it's all we've got. And if my beliefs hold true, then God must *always* be present, in varying guises, whatever is being experienced, posing the perspective then that perhaps duality is only what we perceive as reality, for within God there is only Love. A conundrum, or a koan perhaps, for each of us to ponder, no?

So how does this complete my story of Otter and Dragon? Well, it is a love story after all. My life with Ken, both before and after his physical death, has been about awakening to the power of Love. Finding Ken was my bliss, my heaven on earth. Losing him was my Hell, knocking my very foundations out from under me, dredging up long buried demons causing suffering down to my core. Many years now since his passing, I see that our ongoing journey together has not been unlike that portrayed in What Dreams May Come. How far we have gone to save each other! Finding him again, knowing in my bones that he is still here with me every day, has been an acknowledgment of the magic. What I have come to accept as the ordinary, the commonplace of our communication, is every bit as magical as my SDE the night he "died." And so, the extraordinary has become my ordinary, as a way of life, and it is easy to forget just how magical it is and to have to step back and say WOW now and then. And yet, we are coming into an age where the WOW can become ordinary for all of us. The WOW is instead quickly becoming, OF COURSE!

My journey to this perspective has come to fruition in its own time. Finding my way has been fraught with apprehensions and fears and living small. It has unfolded in an unlikely order and varied contexts, yet it has always led me to the next clue, like any good mystery. There is still much for me to explore about Love and about God, but one thing has been made clear; there is no veil, no dark tunnel, only an unfailing path of Light and Love. Can you see it? It's right over there!

I don't know what my next chapters will look like or how I will find my way, but I do know that at the end of this particular love story, Otter's open arms will be waiting for Dragon once again. My eyes will meet Ken's, and I will feel the touch of his hand as he takes mine and leads me to whatever comes next. And we will go there – together.

Afterword

I always thought
that phoenix birds and resurrections
were things that happened long ago
and far away.

. . .

Ahh, phoenix birds and resurrections
can happen here and now to me and you
and all who dare
to brave the fires of love.

My words in the last chapter may sound like I have found some state of nirvana where my daily life is full of contentment. The truth, of course, is more complicated, and it would be unfair to suggest everything is perfect. Do I still fall in mental and emotional holes after all this? Of course. But I usually scramble out pretty quickly. Sometimes I even see the hole coming and manage to walk around it. And with some ample practice these last few years, I occasionally even walk down a different street.[4]

Do I still miss Ken, long for him sometimes? With regularity. If I could have him back in the physical, in exchange for what I've learned from his death, I would toss these years of learning aside in a nanosecond. I would learn what I needed to learn some other way – with him. But I do see that I have grown and changed and have become more tuned to my soul in the years since his passing because of the journey that ensued.

Could something come along and crush me again? Of course. But my belief is that I would not suffer as I did with Ken's loss. Indeed, I did not with Gwen's.

This is simply the nature of being human. We fall. We get up and try again. And we may go through that falling and getting up sequence

---

[4] This passage about falling into holes is a reference to one of my favorite metaphors. It alludes to a poem by Portia Nelson called "There's a Hole in My Sidewalk" from her book, *The Romance of Self-Discovery*. It's easy to find online; you may enjoy how cleverly it's written.

many times before we stay up. Falling is not failing; it's simply a process. As the actress Mary Pickford said, "You may have a fresh start any moment you choose, for this thing we call failure is not the falling down, but the staying down."

This is also the nature of the spiritual journey. We think we get to the end of some issue and, low and behold, it comes up again and again in a variety of ways, and we are forced to look at it – and look at it – from a different angle every time. The bad news is, we are never done. The good news is, we are never done! It is almost a comfort to know and accept this so you can relax into the repetition and ferret out what is to be learned this time, like any good detective.

The other day, a Facebook friend passed along one of those "Who remembers . . .?" posts, and since I couldn't tell at first what it was about, I was inclined to pass it by. But as I glanced at Ken's smiling picture on my desk, he seemed to be saying, "Open it, sweetheart." It turned out to be a link to a video from *The Shari Lewis Show* where the famous puppet Lamb Chop and all the puppet friends are singing a song – repetitively constructed and circular in nature such that it is a song that never ends. Shari was trying in vain to get them to stop, but since there was no end to the song, of course, they couldn't! If you don't remember the tune, it's easy to find online. But beware. I made the mistake of listening to it, and I've been singing it ever since . . . and giggling a lot. It could be seen as metaphor for my ongoing journey of connection and reconnection with both Ken and Spirit, and so, for me, it is just the greatest little Divine Ditty I've ever heard. I've adopted it as my theme song to the story of Otter and Dragon.

> *This is the song that never ends.*
> *Yes, it goes on and on my friends.*
> *Some people started singing it*
> *Not knowing what it was*
> *And they'll continue singing it forever just because . . .*

> *This is the song that never ends.*
> *Yes, it goes on and on my friends.*
> *Some people started singing it*
> *Not knowing what it was*
> *And they'll continue singing it forever just because . . .*

> *This is the song that never ends*
> *Yes, it goes on and on my friends . . .*

"Expect to have hope rekindled. Expect your prayers to be answered in wondrous ways. The dry seasons in life do not last. The spring rains will come again."

—Sarah Ban Breathnach

Additional Reading

I have referenced several books and websites within the text that marked my way on this spiritual journey. Many others also influenced me and shaped my inquiries, leading me to my own personal discoveries along the path. There are clearly many additional sources of information and support out there as well, and new ones come along every day. I encourage you to explore and find those that call your name. In the meantime, listed below are some of my favorites, including those mentioned in this book, in categories but in no particular order.

Numerology:

- ♥ *Numerology: The Romance in Your Name* by Juno Jordan
- ♥ *Numerology and The Divine Triangle* by Faith Javane & Dusty Bunker
- ♥ *The Life You Were Born to Live* by Dan Millman

Astrology:

- ♥ *New Moon Astrology* by Jan Spiller
- ♥ *The Liquid Light of Sex* by Barbara Hand Clow
- ♥ *The Only Way To Learn Astrology, Volume 1: Basic Principles* by Marion March and Joan McEvers (my copy is really old, like 1980 old, but a good, basic intro nonetheless; there are also a lot of other, newer, good ones out there!)
- ♥ Mark Dodich website: www.astromark.us
- ♥ Paul Nunn's Journey of the Soul Website: www. pauldnunn.com

Dreams:

- ♥ *Dreamgates* by Robert Moss
- ♥ *The Dreamer's Book of the Dead* by Robert Moss

- ♥ Robert Moss Website: www.mossdreams.com
- ♥ *The Mystical Magical Marvelous World of Dreams* by Wilda Tanner

Oracles:

- ♥ *The Book of Runes* by Ralph Blum
- ♥ *The Voyager Tarot* by James Wanless
- ♥ *The Medicine Cards* by Jamie Sams and David Carson
- ♥ *Tarot for Yourself* by Mary Greer
- ♥ *The Faeries Oracle* by Brian Froud and Jessica Macbeth
- ♥ *Mystical Shaman Oracle* by Alberto Villoldo, Colette Baron-Reid, Marcella Lobos

Death, Dying, and the Afterlife:

- ♥ *Reunions* by Raymond Moody, MD
- ♥ *Glimpses of Eternity* by Raymond Moody, MD
- ♥ *Power of the Soul* by John Holland
- ♥ Austyn Wells Website: www.AustynWells.com
- ♥ *Never Letting Go* by Mark Anthony
- ♥ *Proof of Heaven* by Eben Alexander
- ♥ *On Death & Dying* by Elizabeth Kubler Ross
- ♥ *Living Your Dying* by Stanley Keleman
- ♥ SDE Website: www.SharedCrossing.com
- ♥ *At Heaven's Door* by William Peters
- ♥ Conferences: www.IANDS.org
- ♥ *Illuminating the Afterlife* by Cindi Dale
- ♥ *Many Lives, Many Masters* by Brian Weiss, MD
- ♥ *What Tom Sawyer Learned from Dying* by Sidney Saylor Farr

Chakras and Energy Healing:

- ♥ *Wheels of Life* by Anodea Judith, PhD
- ♥ *New Chakra Healing* by Cindi Dale
- ♥ *The Book of Chakra Healing* by Liz Simpson
- ♥ *You Can Heal Your Life* by Louise Hay

Animal & Nature Totems:

- ♥ *Animal Speak* by Ted Andrews
- ♥ *Animal-Wise* by Ted Andrews.
- ♥ *Nature Speak* by Ted Andrews (really anything by Ted – he was prolific and insightful; check him out!)
- ♥ *Animal Magick* by D.J. Conway
- ♥ *Dancing With Dragons* by D.J. Conway
- ♥ *Speaking with Nature* by Sandra Ingerman & Llyn Roberts
- ♥ *Medicine Cards* by Jamie Sams & David Carson (an oracle deck but, though limited in number, the animal messages are lovely)
- ♥ *Love Is In the Earth* by Melody (Crystals and Stones)

Novels:

- ♥ *One* by Richard Bach
- ♥ *Illusions* by Richard Bach
- ♥ *The Alchemist* by Paulo Coelho (and anything by Coelho)
- ♥ *The Barn Dance* by James Twyman

General/Spiritually Oriented:

- ♥ *Anam Cara* by John O'Donohue
- ♥ *The Artist's Way* by Julia Cameron
- ♥ *The Spirituality of Imperfection* by Ernest Kurtz & Katherine Ketcham
- ♥ *Anatomy of the Spirit* by Carolyn Myss

- ♥ *Sacred Contracts* by Carolyn Myss
- ♥ *The Way of the Peaceful Warrior* by Dan Millman
- ♥ *Tomorrow's God* by Neale Donald Walsch
- ♥ *When Everything Changes, Change Everything* by Neale Donald Walsch
- ♥ *Be Happy* by Robert Holden
- ♥ *Polishing the Mirror* by Ram Dass
- ♥ *Red Hot and Holy* by Sera Beak
- ♥ *The Gift of Change* by Marianne Williamson
- ♥ *Help, Thanks, Wow* by Anne Lamott
- ♥ *Women Rowing North* by Mary Pipher
- ♥ *Making Life Easy* by Christiane Northrup, MD
- ♥ *The Invitation; The Call; The Dance; What We Ache For* by Oriah Mountain Dreamer
- ♥ *The Ultimate Brain, Freedom to Change*, a meditation CD by Tom Kenyon
- ♥ *Radical Self-Forgiveness*, book & CD by Colin Tipping
- ♥ *Getting Unstuck*, a CD by Pema Chodron
- ♥ *Guided Meditations for Self-Healing*, a CD by Jack Kornfield
- ♥ *Putting the Giants to Sleep* by David Sheinkin, MD
- ♥ *The Romance of Self-Discovery* ("There's A Hole in My Sidewalk") by Portia Nelson
- ♥ *The Exquisite Risk, Daring to Live An Authentic Life* by Mark Nepo
- ♥ *The Dove in Downward Flight* by Roseanne Farano

Epigraphs

The poetic verse at the start of each chapter is by Gwendolyn Jansma, cited as follows:

- ♥ Chapter 1: "Aftermath" in *Inverted Trees*
- ♥ Chapter 2: excerpted from "Comfort" in *Inverted Trees*
- ♥ Chapter 3: excerpted from "Coming Home" in *The Blessed Ordinary—Wounds and Healings*
- ♥ Chapter 4: "The Force of Yearning" in *Sticks and Stones and Strawberries*
- ♥ Chapter 5: "Invocation" in *Ordinary Magic and Other Ceremonies*
- ♥ Chapter 6: "Illusion" in *Ordinary Wisdom and Other Treasures*
- ♥ Chapter 7: "Lizard Wisdom" in *Sticks and Stones and Strawberries*
- ♥ Chapter 8: "Procession" in *Arrows To The Heart*
- ♥ Chapter 9: "The Key" in *Ordinary Wisdom and Other Treasures*
- ♥ Chapter 10: "Rhythm of Life" in *Gwenana—Her Words*
- ♥ Afterword: excerpted from "Wedding Day" in *Ordinary Magic and Other Ceremonies*

Printed in the United States
by Baker & Taylor Publisher Services